How To
Answer
Interview
Questions-II

101 NEW Q&A

© Copyright Peggy McKee, 2017

Peggy McKee

About the Author

Peggy McKee is an expert resource and a dedicated advocate for job seekers in every step of the job search process—from resumes to interviews to getting the job offer. As CEO of Career Confidential, she educates job  seekers, providing strategies and tools for a fast, wildly successful job search. So far, Career Confidential has helped over 24,000 people in 90 countries get hired fast.

Career Confidential's website, http://CareerConfidential.com, offers more than 100 products, tools, and webinars and apps for job seekers. In addition, Peggy has authored several e-books available through Amazon's Kindle Store. More than 10,000 people attend Career Confidential's free job search and interview webinars every month, and over 1 Million people around the world have downloaded her materials. Peggy receives positive responses every day from candidates who have used them to land the job of their dreams, and she loves that she's been able to contribute to their success.

Peggy McKee has 15+ years of experience in sales, management, recruiting, and career coaching. She believes that her experience has led to her unique advice and unparalleled success rate. Recognized as a job search authority, Peggy has been named #1 on the list of the Top 25 Most Influential Online Recruiters by HR Examiner, and has been quoted in articles from CNN, CAP TODAY, Yahoo!HotJobs, and the Denver Examiner.

Contents

Discuss your resume.

Do you know anyone who works for us?

Does a company need B players? Or is it better off only having A players on staff, and why?

Give an example of a political situation you've dealt with on the job.

Give an example of how you set goals and achieve them.

Give an example of how you were able to motivate employees or co-workers.

Give an example of how you worked on a team.

Have you ever fired someone?

Have you had to turn an employee with a bad attitude into one with a good attitude?

How did you hear about this position?

How did you prepare for this interview?

How do I rate as an interviewer?

I see you had an internship. Did you pursue a full-time job with them? What happened?

If I were to ask your current boss to tell me one thing you do that drives them crazy, what would they say?

If I were to ask your current boss what your greatest strength is, what would they say?

If you are employed, how are you managing time to interview?

If you could choose any company to work for, which one would it be?

If you get the job, how could you lose or make money for me?

If you knew things at your company were rocky, why didn't you get out sooner?

If you were at a business lunch and you ordered a rare steak and they brought it to you well-done, what would you do?

If you were running a company that produces X and the market was tanking for that product, what would you do?

If you were the CEO of this company, what are the top 2 things you would do?

If you won the lottery, would you still work?

your productivity?

What will your job references say about you?

What would the person who likes you least in the world say about you?

What would you do if management made a decision you didn't agree with?

What would you do if you found out the company you worked for was doing something illegal?

What would you do if you got behind schedule with your part of a project?

What would you do if you made an important business decision and a co-worker challenged it?

What would you look to accomplish in the first 30 days/60 days/90 days on the job?

What would your direct reports say about you?

What, as an organization, can we offer that is better than your current employer?

What's your favorite dish, and how would you convince someone who hated an ingredient in it to try it?

Job Interview Question 1

Are you a leader or a follower?

This is an important interview question meant to measure your personality, and how your personality will fit with this particular job.

To answer this question well, it's important to think about what role you are interviewing for. If you are interviewing for **a leadership role** and you say that you are a follower, you probably won't get that job. If you are interviewing for a role where you would be **part of a team** (not the leader) and you say that you are always the leader, you won't be a good fit for the team because you can't work collaboratively.

You might be tempted to knee-jerk reply to this one: "I'm a leader!" In our society, we tend to revere the ideal of the decisive, powerful leader. However, the truth is that **most**

jobs require you to be a little of both. We are (as a society) moving more and more toward collaborative efforts with more fluid lines of leadership. You might easily at various times be part of a team, reporting to a higher-up, leading a team, or heading a project. That doesn't mean that your best answer is always a safe "I'm both." Think about THIS particular job and what it requires to function and be successful.

Whatever your answer, **be prepared to give them an example** of how you have done that.

STAR Format

The STAR format is a great way to help you structure your answers to interview questions when you need to give an example. It helps you include everything you need to in your answer:

Situation or **T**ask - This is whatever was going on at the time. What were you faced with? What was going on? Set the scene.

Action you took - What did YOU do to affect this situation?

Results - Always, always **finish the story by telling them what happened as a result of your actions**. This is the most important part!

If you are a leader, tell them about a time you exercised leadership, including the **actions** you took and what the **results** were. This could be an example of:

- **Spearheading** a multi-piece project that would demonstrate your project management skills

- How you **motivated** a group to achieve a goal

- How you had to make a **hard decision** (telling what the circumstances were and what the results were)

Just like in your resume, **quantify** what you're describing wherever possible:

"I led 12 people in a 6-department project where our job was to streamline processes between departments to save time and money. We decided to (X, Y, and Z) and as a result, cut an average of 2 weeks out of each process and saved each of the 6 departments an average of $100,000 a year."

If you are a follower, help them see **how you contributed** to and **benefited** the team. Employers need followers in many roles, but they like to see followers who can take initiative. Talk about a successful project and what your role in that was—something you did that had a significant impact on the outcome. If you can **quantify that impact**, that's even better:

"My action resulted in a time savings for us, so we got it done 8 days faster."

Or, talk about your overall responsibilities and how your contributions ensured **consistently successful outcomes.**

Are you better at "managing up" or "managing down"?

Are you better at managing up or managing down? Your answer **always needs to be, "I'm good at both."**

Managing up or down is all about extreme **communication skills.** Here's how this works:

If I **manage up** well, then:

✓ I **spend time** with and **talk** with my manager
✓ I understand what their **goals and objectives** are and make those mine, as well
✓ I keep my manager **informed of my progress** on any given project so that they have confidence that things are moving forward toward success
✓ I know what their **expectations** are and make it my

job to **exceed** them

✓ I am **proactive** and try to come up with ideas and solutions to help the organization succeed. I can't do those things if I don't communicate well with my manager.

If I **manage down** well, then:

✓ I am a **good team leader** and a fantastic **communicator**
✓ I understand what our **goals** are and how the team works within the framework to achieve those goals
✓ I choose **great people**
✓ I **clarify our team goals** for them and give them room to achieve
✓ I ask for **input** and I **listen**
✓ I keep the team **moving toward the goal**

Everyone in an organization needs to be good at both—you report to your manager, who reports to the Vice-President, who reports to the President, who reports to the CEO, who reports to the Board of Directors, who report to investors.

You might have direct reports that you need to manage, but even if you don't, you will have times when you are leading a project and need to manage that team for that project.

So, say that you are good at both managing up and managing down, and **give examples** of times when you have done both of those things.

Your answer should be in the form of a **story**: This is what the situation was, this is what happened, this is what I did, this is how it worked out, and this is what the results were.

Use the **STAR** format:

- **S**ituation or **T**ask (Set up the story—what happened? What was your goal?)
- **A**ction (What did you choose to do and why?)
- **R**esult (What happened as a result of your actions? Quantify this wherever possible.)

See the two examples below.

For managing up:

"My manager's goal for the year was X, and my job was Y. We met weekly to discuss results and plan for the next week. At the end of the year, we had achieved our goal, plus 20%, and our department received recognition from the company."

For managing down:

"I was handpicked to put together a team tasked to do X. I chose 5 people from a cross-department pool, set X goals, and met with them daily for a 15-minute meeting to touch base and answer questions. In 3 months, we met 3 goals and exceeded expectations on the other 2 by X."

Are you willing to travel?
(How much are you willing to travel?)

If your answer is an unqualified "yes," because you're willing to go wherever, whenever, for however long it takes, then say so. Any other answer ("maybe," "it depends," "I'd rather not") needs to **wait** until you ask:

> "How much travel is required for this job?
> Can you tell me about that?"

Always ask what the travel expectations actually are before you rule yourself out. I've had great candidates say, "I'm not willing to travel," and then they find out how great the job is, or that the travel is to someplace they're really interested in, or that the salary would be very generous to compensate for all of the travelling, and then, all of a sudden they are willing to travel. If they've already let the company know they aren't willing to travel, they've knocked themselves out of consideration and it's over.

As a recruiter, I can tell you one of the things I found interesting about this question is that people define "travel" very differently.

- Is it **overnight** travel, or is it just **day** travel?
- Do they mean 20% travel, 50% travel, or 90% travel?
  - o If they tell you that it's "50% travel", what does that actually mean in practical terms?
  - o Does it mean you're out Monday, Tuesday and Wednesday every week?
  - o Does it mean you're in the office one week and out the next?

Get specifics, not just percentages, because those can be a cause of miscommunication. Ask how many nights away per week they're talking about, so you are absolutely clear on what they are asking for.

Companies know that people quit jobs over too much travel, so they are sensitive to that as a big factor in whether you'll be happy on the job or not and stay long-term. It's in their best interests to make sure exactly whether or not you are OK with travel. You can help them by asking them to **be clear** on how much travel they are requiring.

It may be that once you find out what they mean by "travel" that you really are not interested in the job—but you'll never know until you ask, so don't rule yourself out until you do.

Assume you come to work here. One year from now you think this is the best job you've ever had. What happened to make you feel that way?

If you ask others about the best job they've ever had, they almost never mention money. (If they do, it's in relation to "I made great money while I was having fun!")

The hiring manager wants to know that you're excited about THIS job, working for THIS company. They want to know that your expectations are clear and align with what you will find here, and that you have their big-picture goals in mind, too.

Does your **vision** for the perfect job match with what their job will actually be like? Will you **enjoy** this job (and stick around in it, creating success) or will you get frustrated and leave? Do you expect to be **successful,** and why?

You have two options here:

(1) Think about what will be the most **rewarding** parts of this job for you, and talk about those. Focus on what THIS company can do or be for you that others can't. At least part of your answer should focus on that **you'll be happy because they'll be happy:**

"I'll know I'm using my skills in X, Y, and Z to significantly help boost our company's growth/market share/profit and I'll be excited and happy about that."

(2) Refer to the **job goals** you may have talked about already and talk about how you've **achieved** those (in a year).

"I will have accomplished X, Y, and Z, that you said were our primary goals, and …."

Answer either way, incorporate job accomplishments and your personal goals and desires, and focus on your success.

Remember that if you're receiving a paycheck, you're achieving a quantifiable goal. That's the only reason a company would hire anyone. So tie your goals and objectives to **quantifiable goals** the company needs to accomplish. For instance, if you know that the company wants to accomplish "X" in a year, you would say that at the end of the year you would have achieved that goal for them and felt a great sense of accomplishment because you did so.

Relate your answer to what they need, but be **sincere** about what would make THIS company a fun place for you to work. Your enthusiasm will show, and make you more attractive to this employer.

Describe a time when you were asked to do something you weren't trained to do. How did you handle it?

This is a fantastic behavioral interview question that gets at the heart of **how you respond to challenges**. How do you think about them—are you **afraid or excited**? Do you have the **initiative** to tackle something new? How do you **approach the task**? Can you **think critically** and make good, logical decisions? How do you **function without structure**? In your answer, talk about:

- **resources** you used
- **mentors** you called
- **books** you read
- **counterparts** you spoke with
- **audio** you listened to
- YouTube **videos** you watched
- **coaches** you contacted

How did you train yourself
to successfully accomplish the task?

Use the **STAR** format:

- **S**ituation or **T**ask (Set up the story—what happened? What was your goal?)
- **A**ction (What did you choose to do and why?)
- **R**esult (What happened as a result of your actions? Quantify this wherever possible.)

Here are some sample answers:

****

"X was the situation, and I remembered that I had done something similar in Y, so I did a little research online and figured out how to apply the principles I learned there to achieve this new goal."

****

"I was faced with X, and at first, I didn't know what to do. But I remembered that our overall goals were A, B, and C. So I thought about what course of action would keep us moving toward those goals? After that, it was easy to narrow down the options, and this is what I did. As a result, we had a fantastic outcome, XYZ."

****

"In my last job, X happened. We had no procedures in place to handle that, so I did some research and found some books on the subject. I read those, had a couple of discussions with my mentor, to kick around ideas, and presented my ideas to my team. After some discussion with them, I developed a new set of procedures to handle X. We had such success with it that the company implemented our new procedure throughout all the divisions."

****

"In my first job, X happened. I didn't know the first thing about how to handle it, so I did some research and asked for input from people in a similar position with more experience than I had at that time. I was able to use some of what they told me and incorporated it into a new solution for our problem. As a result, we saw X% increase in sales."

****

The hiring manager wants to know that you can **think on your own** and come up with rational, proactive **solutions** that produce great results for the company.

Describe a time when your team did not agree.

The cooperation of countless people on teams is how business is done. Yet, no team always gets along perfectly. When that happens, what do you do? How do you handle conflict? Can you lead others to consensus?

Conflict resolution is an important skill. How you deal with any conflict says a lot about you, your personality, and your professionalism.

This question can pertain either to a team that you led (how do you manage people who disagree?), or to a team that you are on (can you mediate between team members and exercise leadership even if you weren't assigned as leader?).

Always, when asked to describe any situation in an interview question, use the **STAR** format:

- **S**ituation or **T**ask (Set up the story—what happened? What was your goal?)
- **A**ction (What did you choose to do and why?)
- **R**esult (What happened as a result of your actions? Quantify this wherever possible.)

Ideally, your story should tell about how you:

- **asked questions** to achieve understanding
- found **common ground**
- **presented data** for the decision-making process
- realized a **productive or profitable outcome**

Lots of people will tell the story but forget to mention the outcome. **The outcome, or result, of your actions, is what the employer cares about most.** (Include the actual numbers in the story as much as you can—quantification is powerful.)

If your example is a team that you led:

Situation or Task – Briefly set up the situation that led to the conflict. Choose something that was an **actual problem** involving priorities or a budget. (Don't talk about trivial things, like how the team couldn't agree on where to go to lunch.) **Be brief.** The employer doesn't need to know that much about the details.

Action – How did you approach the team? How did you exercise your leadership? Talk about how you listened (listening is a critical skill), taking into account the emotions of the people on your team, and made a **rational, logical decision** (rather than one based on your own emotions).

Result – This is your real focus here—the **outcome**. What happened as a direct result of your actions? This is a prime spot to **add numerical evidence** for the employer ("As a result of my plan, we were able to reduce overlap by 50%, which also drastically reduced the time spent in X.").

If your example is a team that you were on (but not necessarily leading), you want to:

- Talk about how you **mediated** the conflict, again by listening and taking the emotion out of the equation.

- Describe how you took the time to **talk** to each member of the team and hear what they had to say.

- Talk about how you **rooted out the miscommunication** or found common ground.

- End with what happened as a **result**—always a **positive** one.

So you might say,

"I was part of a handpicked cross-department Kaizen team tasked to find ways to become more lean and efficient as a company. But some of the suggestions stepped on the toes of one person in particular who was from X area and caused them to react badly. I took them out for coffee to take some of the group pressure off and we talked. I discovered the real problem and helped them present their issue to the group in a different way. As a group, we came up with a new solution that made this person feel much more positive about it and still achieved our goal. The end result was that we were able to streamline X number of procedures and save the company as a whole about 40 hours a week, which they valued at $X."

Describe a time you reduced costs or improved efficiency.

Every single one of our jobs is tied to **money**. Companies are in business to make money, and every cog in the machine needs to work smoothly together toward that goal. If you don't make more money than you cost, you won't hold your job very long.

So, there must be a time when you reduced costs or improved efficiency in any job you've done, and you need to pinpoint what it is and quantify it. (**Quantifying** it means to identify the numbers that describe the savings—you saved 3 hours, you saved $300, you improved it by 30%, etc.)

Here's an example of a gentleman with a great answer to this:

He was working on a machine, with gold wires. In his process, excess gold was actually falling on the floor—very tiny pieces, as scrap. He went to his supervisor and said, "Look, we should not be throwing away these scraps. We should be figuring out a way to get that gold out of those shavings and recycle it for our sales or for something else.

The supervisor thought that was a great idea, so they actually started keeping those shavings and trying how to figure out a way to separate the gold from the other material—and they did. The company rewarded him with a sizable bonus.

This is a great story because it proved that he is someone who takes **initiative**, thinks in a **bigger-picture way** about the company, and can **bring solutions** above and beyond what his job requires—but what makes it better is **quantifying** it. How would he do that?

He would know how much those gold reels cost: $200, $1000, $100,000, $200,000, or whatever it is. Maybe the shavings represent a 10 % loss, and this idea recovered that for the company.

Whatever the numbers are, you should know so you can describe the **money you saved or the efficiency you improved**. Think it all the way through.

Whatever your job is, think about what you have done that **saved time, saved money, improved efficiency, and reduced costs**. It all adds up to a financial benefit for the company that helps to justify the cost of hiring you—your salary. When you talk about it in your interview, they will be thinking that if you did that for another company, you can do that for their company, too.

Key to a Great Interview!

Any story like this where you received a reward or other recognition is fantastic for your Brag Book.

Your Brag Book (aka professional portfolio) is evidence that you can do what you say you can do. Show specific pages to illustrate an answer to an interview question, or show it as a general example of the quality of your work. It sets you apart as someone who pays attention to details, is achievement-oriented, and cares about giving your best. It's definitely a "wow" factor.

To the hiring manager, hiring you often feels like a risk. Brag books are another way to make them feel more comfortable hiring you.

If you haven't already, start putting your brag book together today. You'll be amazed at how much it helps your interview performance.

If you would like help putting yours together, check out

Career Confidential's
Brag Book eReport on Amazon

amazon.com

Describe a work or school instance where you messed up.

Everybody makes mistakes. You know it, and the interviewer knows it and they will always ask you about them. Why?

(1) They want to reveal your **character**. Are you someone who admits making a mistake or who blames it on others? Are you too perfect to even think of a mistake you made? Or maybe you have such low self-esteem that you can think of hundreds of things that were all your fault.

(2) They want to know if you **learn from your mistakes** and come out of them better than you were before. Or do you keep repeating the same mistakes over and over again?

Think of a time you made a mistake and acted in the situation so that it ended on a positive note.

What are the 'rules' of a good mistake story?

Don't talk about the biggest mistake you ever made that spiraled out of control and had huge repercussions for your company.

If your story takes 3 minutes because of all the times you say, "and THEN this terrible thing happened", you are choosing the wrong story.

Don't talk about a mistake that points to a major flaw.

If you are an accountant, don't talk about the time you transposed a number and didn't catch it until your manager was in the middle of a presentation to the CEO—talk about the time you had a miscommunication with a co-worker and how you talked it out and improved your communication skills with co-workers.

If you're an administrative assistant, don't talk about the time you failed to communicate vital information and caused your boss to miss an important meeting—talk about the time in your first job that you didn't write down a message because you thought you could remember it and you didn't, and you had to call back, so now you are meticulous about keeping information complete and organized.

Choose a small, work-related mistake that was a problem for you, but not necessarily the company.

Tell what you did to rectify the mistake or address the shortcoming that caused it in the first place.

Show that you improved as a result of the mistake—that you had a growth experience that made you better at your job.

Describe how you would complete [a typical task on this job].

This behavioral interview question is very job-specific, so the details of your answer depend on the job itself. The primary reason they're asking this is to make sure you're what you say you are, and you **understand what the job is** and what you have to do to be **successful** at it. However, they also want an insight into your **thinking style** and **problem-solving skills**, and this question helps them get to that.

Think about this before you answer it. Break up whatever task it is into 5-10 steps and walk them through the steps.

"If I were going to do this, here's what I would do: [1, 2, 3, 4, and 5]. I would involve X person in this, and let Y person know. I would have ABC contingency plan just in case."

HINT!

Take paper and pen to your job interviews!

Use it to sketch out ideas to help yourself think and better answer interview questions.

Take notes for your thank you note and second interview.

After you walk them through it, you should ask, "Was that correct?" **Ask if you answered the way they were looking for, or if there was something you're missing.** Ask if they would like you to explain anything further.

Clarifying for understanding is something you especially need to do with these types of questions, so that you are sure you answered it to their satisfaction before you move on.

If they communicate to you that your answer wasn't what they were looking for, **ask what you were missing**. Turn it into a learning moment. Have this conversation with them and think it through. They'll get a chance to see how your mind works, and see what it would be like if they were working with you and showing you how to do things on the job.

Communication like this, with interaction, is at a higher level, and it will show someone that you are very **confident, interested, and flexible,** and these are all good things that you want your potential employer to know about you.

Key to a Great Interview!

This question is a perfect time to introduce your
30-60-90-day plan!

**Find out more about 30-60-90-Day Plans
at http://CareerConfidential.com.**

Describe the boss who could get the very best work from you.

This question is looking at **fit**—how you'll fit into the organizational culture, and how you'll fit with the person who would be your boss. Your answer shows your personality, your work style, and your communication skills. It also sheds light on your past relationships.

I would say, "I always give my best work, no matter what. But I would enjoy a boss who...."

Or, "I always give my best work, no matter what, but I've had some great bosses over the years that really inspired me because..."

It's important to note that **you always give your best**, no matter what the circumstances around you are. And then just point out **2-3 things you particularly enjoy** in someone who supervises your work.

The key here is balance:

- You want to be honest, because you don't want to say you love being micro-managed if you really hate it, because it would affect you and your work negatively.

- But you also don't want to pin yourself down to a specific list of 'must-haves' in case this person doesn't have them all. Even if you'd be fine working without them, now they feel that you'd be unhappy and a bad fit.

If you are talking about a **future boss**, a nice safe thing to do is to mention **2-3 qualities that are broad enough to fit many people**, and that managers strive for as a general rule:

- "I love a boss who **communicates** with me on a regular basis, letting me know **expectations and goals**."

- "I love a boss who **knows a lot about the industry**, because I can learn so much from them."

- "I love a boss who **trusts me** enough to let me work independently but **helps me** when I need it."

If you talk about a **boss who inspired you in the past**, mention something they did that helped you be successful in the job, or made you better, stronger, or more effective than you were before:

- "I always give my best work, no matter what, but I've had some great bosses over the years that really inspired me. One in particular was a time management genius, and she really showed me how to learn to prioritize my tasks in order to manage my time and increase my productivity."

(Give a specific example of this, with **quantification** of how much your productivity increased.) Your example could be a boss who taught you organization, communication, management skills, or anything else that has resulted in you being better at your job.

Key to a Great Interview - Quantification

Describe your achievements in terms of **numbers, dollars, and percentages.** See how **quantification strengthens your answer:**

- "I brought in new clients" or
  "Brought in 20 new clients in 3 months"

- "I delivered product on time and under budget" or
  "98% on-time delivery of product"

- "Maintained accuracy in company database" or
  "100% accuracy in 50,000-item database over 2 years"

Discuss your educational background.

This seems straightforward, and in one sense, it is—your educational background is a fact. However, there's always a difference between giving a straightforward interview answer and giving **a *job-winning* interview answer**.

If your **degree is obviously related** to the job you're interviewing for, say, "My undergraduate is in Chemistry and I have an MBA. What else would you like to know?"

Asking a question in return keeps the conversation going, which is what you want in an interview. Maybe they want to know why you chose this field. If it were me, I'd say:

"I chose Chemistry because I like it, and because not many people go into Chemistry so I knew it would make me stand out. Plus, I knew that as a female, a Chemistry degree would make me stand out even more, because it's unusual. I went on to get the MBA because I knew that the Chemistry degree plus the MBA would make me even more valuable and better at my job. I'm always looking for educational experiences that help me with that goal. Some people would get the MBA because they think it would naturally get them paid more, just because they hold it. I never thought of it that way. My opinion was, if I get an MBA, I'll be better at my job—and the value I bring is what will get me paid more for the work that I do."

If your degree is not 100% related to the job you're applying for, then connect those dots for them:

"My degree is in Psychology, which gives me a unique perspective to bring to this job that most people in this field don't have, so I can bring fresh, out-of-the-box thinking along with an understanding of what makes people tick, and I have excellent communication skills."

If you got a minor (or even just a few classes) in something more directly related and helpful to the job you're applying for, mention those:

"My degree is in Philosophy, but I took 3 classes in X that I did very well in and led me to pursue this as a career. The skills I developed in those classes, backed by the solid critical-thinking skills I honed in my major make me especially effective in this arena."

"Education" is not limited to formal classes at a college or university. You can also count:

- **certification / training** classes (work-sponsored or not)
- **programs** you participated in
- **mentorships** with someone in your field
- even **reading** you've done on your own (being 'self-taught' can be even more impressive, because it shows your level of drive and commitment)

Discuss your resume.

This is a standard, open-ended interview question a lot like, "Tell me about yourself." They just want you to walk them through your resume. Your job is to be a tour guide, giving them the relevant facts they will be most interested in as they consider you for this job.

Start from your education and go forward, rather than starting with your most recent job. So, say something like, "Well, my resume is in reverse chronological order, starting with my most recent experience, but let me start from the beginning and go forward. I went to X school and got a degree in Y. My first job was at ABC."

From there, **it's important to have thought about this job** that you are interviewing for and **what parts of your story will be most impressive** to this interviewer.

"From there, I was promoted to X position, where I accomplished Y."

"From there, I went to Acme Corporation as an X, where I was awarded ABC."

"From there, I went to XYZ Company where I honed my skills in A, B, C so that I could move up to [a promotion]."

What you mention as your accomplishment, the award you won, and the skills you honed **should have as much to do with your ability to succeed at THIS job as humanly possible.** For instance, you wouldn't bother mentioning a Customer Service Award if the job you're interviewing for will have you never speaking to a customer. As great as that may be, mentioning it will throw the hiring manager off track, and make them see you as a Customer Service person who probably wouldn't fit well into this role.

If you have a job in your history that seems **out of place,** or **that you were in a very short time,** or anything else that might cause questions, now's the time to **explain your thinking** behind taking/leaving that position, or taking that time off, or whatever it is. Explain how it fit with your overall career path, or how it was a one-time mistake you learned from or circumstance that won't happen again.

Be strategic. Think about which parts of your story would make them want to hire you. And always think about what could be described in **numbers, dollars, or percentages** ("I worked there for 6 months when I was promoted as a result of a program I started that saved $ per year").

Do you know anyone who works for us?

Many times, the answer to this question is 'yes,' because many of us find out about jobs or get our foot in the door with the help of someone we know.

If they ask you this question, it's probably because they are thinking about asking for **references**. Someone they know (such as someone who works at their company) is going to be a much stronger reference for you than someone they don't.

If you know someone who works in this company, this someone **needs to have an excellent reputation** within the company. If you know that's the case, then go ahead and tell the interviewer who they are. They will associate you with that person they love and you will be in a better position to get the offer. But after you mention this person, bring it back to why you'd be a good fit. For example:

"Yes, I know John Smith. We've worked well together before, and he encouraged me to apply here. Because of that, I did some research on my own, and the more I found out about your company, the more I got excited about the idea of working here, because I believe this is a place where I could really contribute to growth with my skills in X, Y, and Z."

If the person you know is someone having problems, you might not want to mention them because you will be associated with their negative qualities. Or, you can mention them with a caveat:

"I do know John Smith, but that wasn't a factor in my applying here. I applied because I believe that my skills in A, B, and C are a perfect fit for this job, and the more I have learned about the company and your plans for the future, the more excited I am about the possibility of working here."

If you don't know anyone who works for them, then answer the question behind the question (they are interested in your references):

"No, I don't know anyone who works here, but I can absolutely provide you with references, if that's what you're interested in. They can speak to my skill set, work ethic, and value as an X to your company."

Does a company need B players? Or is it better off only having A players on staff, and why?

A vs B

Any answer to this question other than "A players" means that you are not an A player. **A players like to work with A players.**

I don't know any managers who should be looking for B players. You should always hire the best you can get, and that's an A player. The more A players you have, the more growth and movement you have.

The more A players you have, the more cushion you have in case one of your A players leaves for a better opportunity.

It doesn't make sense to look for B players anyway—in any organization, there will be some who naturally keep their A player status, and some that will land in B or fall into C status.

That's not to say that B players can't be valuable to an organization. They can. They are often the backbone of an organization that can keep the daily details moving—but they tend not to contribute to active growth.

Key to a Great Interview

For more on 'A' and 'B' players, read Brad Smart's book –
Topgrading, 3rd Edition: The Proven Hiring and Promoting Method That Turbocharges Company Performance

It talks about how hiring managers should always try to get A players, because there will be enough of them that fall to B player status. If you're going to be a manager, you need to read this book.

Give an example of a political situation you've dealt with on the job.

Office politics are the "people" part of getting things done at work. Every organization is made up of individuals with varying power levels, goals, relationship lines, and personal emotional baggage they carry with them every day.

This question gets at your **interpersonal**, **communication**, and **conflict-resolution** skills. How do you bring your **emotional intelligence** into play to navigate in situations brimming with the baggage and hidden agendas of the various players?

Maybe even more importantly, can you do this **without bringing your own emotional baggage or reactions** to the situation? This shows your **maturity, self-control and level of professionalism**.

A 'difficult' political situation is going to be one where **the balance of power is not in your favor**. Your example needs to be one where you **exercised diplomacy or tact** to not just come out unharmed, but ideally to make all the players satisfied with the outcome (everybody wins).

So, a great story to tell might be the time you were involved in a **group project** where one member kept throwing up roadblocks that angered the rest of the group, so you took that person aside, asked questions, found areas of agreement, came back in, built consensus, and got the project done.

As much as you can, **keep the story you choose to tell positive**, with you in a **mediator role** rather than in the direct line of fire.

You don't want to talk about how you had to distance yourself from your boss because the CEO hated him, and walk the tightrope until you could get out of Dodge.

You don't want to talk about how your boss wanted you to do something unethical, and you had to tactfully get out of doing it.

Stories like those are too negative, too gossipy, and don't accomplish the goal of every interview answer you give: to show your fit for the job.

Keep it positive and show how you made a positive impact on the situation.

Give an example of how you set goals and achieve them.

This is a softball behavioral interview question. You have the power to **choose a story that highlights your very best selling qualities** for this job—so use it wisely. Show them how you think, how you approach problems and goals, and how you can succeed. Always choose a **professional example, NOT a personal one**. Choose a story that relates as much as possible to a **skill that is central to this job**, so that they can easily see how your success in this story would transfer to success in this job.

A good goal that you reached could be anything:

- **Completing** an important project

- **Gaining** a key customer
- **Improving** a system or process
- **Increasing** sales
- **Reducing** employee turnover
- **Implementing** new procedures to improve X
- **Improving** the company's reputation for customer service

Tell your story using a **STAR** format:

- **S**ituation or **T**ask (Set up the story— what happened? What was your goal?)
- **A**ction (What did you choose to do and why?)
- **R**esult (What happened as a result of your actions? Quantify this wherever possible.)

For example:

Situation –

"I was assigned X project. It was a complicated project with lots of moving parts, and had to be completed in 90 days."

Task or Action –

"I set a goal of getting the project done in 80 days so we'd have time to make corrections or deal with problems that came up along the way. To keep things running as efficiently as possible, I assigned parts of the project to 5 different teams, with check-in meetings every week. I was able to coordinate their tasks and minimize downtime."

Result –

"Because of the way I set it up, we completed the project on time and 10% under budget. Our Vice-President was so impressed, I received a company award and presented my process at the next company meeting so that other managers could learn from it and implement it, too."

Your story should clearly demonstrate how you added value to the organization through your actions.

Use **numbers, dollars, or percentages** to quantify this added value and add a lot of strength to your answer.

Key to a Great Interview - Quantification

Describe your achievements in **numbers, dollars, and percentages**. See how it **strengthens your answer**:

- "I brought in new clients" or
  "Brought in 20 new clients in 3 months"

- "I delivered product on time and under budget" or
  "98% on-time delivery of product"

- "Maintained accuracy in company database" or
  "100% accuracy in 50,000-item database over 2 years"

**Numbers, dollars, or percentages answer the hiring manager's (interviewer's) primary question:
"How can this person benefit MY company?"**

Give an example of how you were able to motivate employees or co-workers.

To motivate someone, you need to know them—what motivates one won't motivate another. To know them, you must be a **good communicator.**

Communication is a vital skill. How you communicate and motivate says a lot about your work style and management style.

Tell your story using a **STAR** format:

- **S**ituation or **T**ask (Set up the story— what happened? What was your goal?)
- **A**ction (What did you choose to do and why?)
- **R**esult (What happened as a result of your actions? Quantify this wherever possible.)

** If you're interviewing for a **management** position:

Talk about how you **developed relationships** with the members of your team, creating a strong, cohesive unit that was able to **achieve X** (X should be a quantified value, like "the highest sales numbers in the company" or "the award for the best customer service in the division" or whatever outcome you achieved.)

Or, tell how you **developed an accountability/rewards program** that boosted employee performance by X%.

Or, talk about how you go through the process of **setting expectations and providing specific feedback, and what the results of this process are for you.** Choose an example that showcases your successful management style.

** If you're interviewing for a spot on a **team:**

Talk about the time your group had a member who was more focused on **personal issues** than on getting the work done and say what you did to address that issue.

Maybe you created a friendly **competition** to get them engaged.

Or, you asked them out to lunch and **developed a relationship** with them, and you realized that they felt they weren't a valued part of the group, so they weren't participating. When you addressed that issue, the person felt better and became a strong part of the team, and you even became friends.

Any of these kinds of answers show that you are a **team player** who keeps an eye on the group as a whole, not just on your individual piece. It sets you apart as a **leader** they can depend on.

Either way, use the STAR format to talk about your example, and try to **quantify the outcome**.

Give an example of
how you worked on a team.

In your new job, you'll also at some point be required to work with others—even if your job is primarily as an individual contributor. Companies want to know that you can do this and get the job done with a minimum of conflicts and issues.

This question is trying to get at your **people skills**—communication skills and other 'soft' skills that aren't on your resume but that dramatically affect your ability to do your job well.

At some point in your life, you worked on some kind of a team, whether it was an officially-recognized, formal team or simply a loose group with a common goal.

Try to choose a situation that would be similar to one you might experience in this new job, or a situation that uses a skill that is central to your success in this new job.

Tell your story using a **STAR** format:

- **S**ituation or **T**ask (Set up the story—what happened? What was your goal?)
- **A**ction (What did you choose to do and why?)
- **R**esult (What happened as a result of your actions? Quantify this wherever possible.)

The Situation or Task

- What kind of team was it?
- How did you come to be on the team?
- Were you chosen specifically for this team, or was it a normal part of your job?
- What was the goal of the team?
- Were you facing any difficult circumstances?
- Were you on a time limit?
- Were you on a budget?
- Was the team not getting along?
- What was going on?

The Action you took

- What did you choose to do in response to the situation?
- Was this something that you came up with and had to convince others to go along with?
- Explain the thought process behind the decision you made.

The Results you achieved

- What was the outcome of the action?
- Did you get a positive response?
- Was your team recognized for your achievement?
- Can you quantify it?
    - Did you complete your project 5 days ahead of schedule?
    - Did you save $10,000?
    - Did you cut 5 minutes off of every part, so that you saved 80 hours over a year?

What if you're a **student with no work experience interviewing for your first job? How do you answer this question?

There will be some example from your past where you worked on a team—a **group project, a sports team, or even a school play**. Talk about the teamwork that helped you came together to achieve your common goal.

Have you ever fired someone?

If you're interviewing for a management role, they're likely to ask you this question. Managers are usually required to both hire and fire as necessary. They want to know how you would handle that—your **thought process**, how you **feel** about it, and if you can make **good, logical, thoughtful choices** about this situation. Can you make **tough choices**?

If your answer is "No," that you have never fired anyone, you need to follow that up with, "But I always live up to my responsibilities, and I know that this is one that comes with the job, as unpleasant as it might be. Although it is probably difficult to make that decision, I know that I would make it with the good of the whole department and the whole company in mind, with any necessary input from HR and my own supervisor."

You want them to know that **you can make difficult decisions that benefit the greater good**, and that you recognize that the company will have procedures that need to be followed in these situations.

If your answer is "Yes," you'll want to describe what happened.

Tell your story using a **STAR** format:

- **S**ituation or **T**ask (Set up the story—what happened? What was your goal?)
- **A**ction (What did you choose to do and why?)
- **R**esult (What happened as a result of your actions? Quantify this wherever possible.)

For example:

Talk about what was going on with this employee, walk them through the process of how you addressed the situation, and how it ultimately came to firing that person. Mention what happened after that—maybe morale went up because this person was so negative they drug everyone else down, or maybe your production percentages went up because this person wasn't around to gum up the works any longer.

You want them to know that you:

- **didn't take it lightly**
- **went through the proper channels**
- **ultimately made the hard decision and took care of business**

Have you had to turn an employee with a bad attitude into one with a good attitude?

We've all encountered the person who causes trouble—they gossip, bully, or cause dissension; they're disrespectful and uncooperative; they gripe about the company/ workload/ long hours/ ugly office/etc., they spend a lot of time goofing off on Facebook or Pinterest, taking long lunches, calling in sick constantly, or otherwise not pulling their weight.

Some companies want to cut those people loose as soon as possible, but some want to try to save them. After all, there was a reason they were hired in the first place and they'd like to have *that* person. Besides, the process you have to follow can be long and daunting, and hiring someone new is expensive and time-consuming.

If you have a story where you've taken someone like that and turned them around, it shows you as a tremendous **communicator and motivator** — two excellent managerial qualities. They want to see that you can take action when an employee causes a drain on morale or productivity. These things can snowball and ruin a previously well-running program.

Any number of ways you may have approached this situation is good to talk about, **as long as the outcome was positive**:

- The employee was stuck in a job beyond his or her capabilities, so you gave them a personality test, found another position that fit them much better, moved them over, and now everyone is happy and thriving.

- The employee had excellent hard skills but sub-par communication skills, so you sent him to a class to improve and he came back a new person.

- The company made a mistake in a new policy that negatively affected an employee, and they were legitimately angry. You discussed it with them, successfully addressed the issue and they were satisfied.

- Her mother was diagnosed with cancer, so you worked out a flex plan so she could take care of her personal business and still be productive at her job.

- You called them into your office, pointed out their behavior in private, and worked out a Personal Improvement Plan. When they realized how their actions were going to hurt them and maybe even get them fired, they straightened up.

Any story where you assessed the problem, communicated with the employee, came up with a professional, specific, and results-oriented plan of action, executed it and realized success, is a good one to tell here.

How did you hear about this position?

This is probably an opening question, possibly in a phone interview—but that's no reason not to answer it in a powerful way.

Never say, "I saw it on Monster" (or Career Builder, Indeed, etc.) and leave it at that. This makes it seem as if you are trolling for any job, anywhere, and you don't care what it is as long as you get paid for it.

If you did learn about it on a **job board**, say so, but then follow up with what caused you to apply for it: "I realized as I read through the job description that I am the perfect fit for this job."

Or, you were so excited to find it because you're a great fit for the job because of A, B, and C (your skills) AND because it's somewhere you always wanted to live.

Or you were so excited to find it because you've heard great things about this company for a long time and you're thrilled about the possibility of working there.

Add **something that expresses your fit or enthusiasm**, which will set you apart.

If you found out about the job through a more focused source, such as an industry **newsletter**, a **LinkedIn group post**, or on their own **company website**, say so, and then again, add what it was that caused you to be excited about applying for the job.

If you found out about the job through a **friend or professional contact**, tell them who that person is and why they thought of you for the job (which mentions your fit for it). Then you can say, "And as I found out more about the job, I agreed. And, it's even a great fit because of X. I'm so glad my friend called me!"

If you found out through a **recruiter**, this can be the most powerful source of all, because the recruiter is the person who likely has a relationship with the company, and who definitely has the most objective viewpoint on whether or not you're a good candidate for the job. Again, mention why the recruiter thought you were an especially good fit for the job and why you think so, too.

Even with questions that don't really seem on the surface like a serious job interview question, **don't miss the opportunity you have with it (and every question) to sell yourself for the job.**

How did you prepare for this interview?

I LOVE this question. It's an ideal time to **set yourself apart from every other candidate** in a big way.

The **best-prepared candidate is the one who gets the job**, and this is when to show you're that person and make it an easy decision to hire you.

A **'good' answer** would be: "I researched the company" and show that you did by asking great questions about the company, its priorities, and future direction.

A GREAT, stand-head-and-shoulders-above-every-other-candidate, "WOW" answer is to say:

"I'm so glad you asked. I created a **30-60-90-day plan** so you can see how I'd approach the job in my first 90 days and be very successful. I'd like you to have all the information you can about me, and I'd like to find out more about you, so we can see if I'd be a good fit for the position. Can we take a few minutes to go over my plan and see what you think?"

No interviewer will say "No" to this. They will all say "Yes," because **they will be incredibly interested** in what you have done. When you show them your plan, they'll clearly see the level of **preparation** you put into this interview and the level of **professionalism** and commitment that you'd bring to the job.

To complete your plan, you'll have to:

- **Research the company** (your plan should be as specific as possible to that company)
- **Think** about what it takes to be successful in the job
- **Organize** and **prioritize strategies** to execute for that success

Key to a Great Interview!

A 30-60-90-day plan in the BEST preparation
you can do for any job interview!

**Find out more about 30-60-90-Day Plans
at http://CareerConfidential.com.**

Your answers to all their interview questions will be better because of this research.

When you go through your plan, **ask smart, informed questions** about the job. You'll get **priceless feedback** from this manager about what they see as the primary goals for the job, and what they really think of you and your fit for the position. This will be the **best possible preparation** you could do for the interview.

How do I rate as an interviewer?

There are not many places you can easily use **humor** in a job interview, but this answer is one of them: "I'm not sure. If you're going to move me forward, I'm going to give you a 10; if you're not, I'm going to give you a zero."

Some questions (like this one) are designed to throw you off your rehearsed and prepared interview game. They want to see **how you react in an unexpected situation**, and maybe even to see how you handle an **awkward** one (like evaluating the person who is supposed to be evaluating you).

Your **safest bet** (besides using humor) is to **focus on the positive** parts of the interview—maybe the interviewer smiled and put you at ease when you arrived. Maybe they're asking you great questions or making it easy for you to point out how well you'd do in the role.

How do you balance life and work?

This question can be a fishing expedition to see what you'll reveal about yourself that they aren't allowed to ask you directly. Very often, it's the new version of, "Who takes care of your children when they're sick?" They want to know if you're willing to work extra hours, or if you'll be off a lot with personal matters (like sick children), or if you're the kind of person whose desk chair is empty at 5:01 every day, no matter what.

Once in a while, it means that they're actually concerned with your overall health, because they know that a healthy individual is a better contributor who makes better decisions.

Your **best answer** is, **"I am very organized."** You can elaborate by talking about how you fully engage at work and when you get home, you fully engage there—and it wouldn't be a bad idea to talk about how stepping away from work frees your mind so that you often come up with great ideas at home, and keep a notebook handy to jot those down.

You could assume that the employer is asking about what you do in your **spare time** to offset the stress of work, and this would be a good opportunity to mention an **active hobby** such as running, dancing, hiking, tennis, or even traveling, that makes you seem full of energy. I always like to hear candidates talk about how they **take classes** to learn something new, because I believe that is a positive, that you're willing to learn new things.

You might be able to make a connection with the interviewer, if you happen to have the same hobby they do. Play it safe— try to mention common hobbies like running, hiking, etc. rather than unusual ones (like taxidermy).

If you are really unsure about what to say, toss the ball back into their court: "What do other employees here do?" Or, "What do you do?" This will give you an idea of where they are and where you should be aiming when you answer this question.

Keep in mind that even with this question, **every word you say has a purpose—to convince them to hire you.**

 Now's not the time to mention any interest you might have in Flex-Time, Job Sharing, working from home, or any other non-traditional arrangement— unless you know they have a program already in place, or unless it's an absolute deal breaker. Otherwise, wait until they love you and are closer to an offer (or better yet, after you've worked there for a while).

How do you compensate for your weaknesses?

Your interviewer knows that if they ask, "What's your greatest weakness?" you'll have an answer ready that doesn't really seem like a weakness and puts you in good light. Asking this way, "How do you compensate for your weaknesses?" might throw you off your game a bit. It drills a little deeper and assumes that you have a weakness and simply asks what you are doing about it.

Give them a weakness that doesn't affect a central, critical part of your job and tell them what you already do to overcome it.

For instance, I would say that I am not particularly detail-oriented, and that's why I take the extra steps of X, Y, and Z so I don't miss anything.

This might be a good opportunity to show that you are coachable, which is a big plus in the eyes of your future supervisor. Say, "I used to have a problem with X, but my mentor gave me a fantastic solution (then describe that). I've been using it ever since with no problems."

Or, this might be a good opportunity to show that **you can train yourself,** when necessary:

"I used to be a little afraid of technology, but then I signed up for some classes on my own to learn what I needed to. I brush up my skills with a new class every few months or so."

It's going to take some thought on your part, but **be strategic** and think of an answer that names a weakness that is not a deal-breaking factor for this job, and a compensation that highlights a **great quality** they would like to see in you.

Think about the company, think about the job itself, and really tailor your answer to fit.

How do you feel about an income made up totally of commissions?

If they are asking you this question, (1) you know you're interviewing for a sales job; and (2) they're probably going to pay you only commissions, rather than a base plus commissions.

Since **this is a salary question**, your best bet at this point is to just yet. What you're trying to do is move through the process, not knock yourself out of the running by giving the wrong answer.

Your best strategy when faced with this question is to ask questions of your own:

"In the past, my income has been split between base pay, commissions, and bonuses, so I'm not sure. Are all of your positions commissions-only?"

Stay away from what you really think and ask questions to get as much information as you can.

How do you feel about working for a younger manager?

If you're asked this, you're an older worker. Job seekers over 50 (sometimes, over 40) have a reputation for not being able to take orders from some young whippersnapper.

Help them feel better about hiring you, by saying a definitive, "I'd be fine with that. No problem." To lend yourself additional credibility, add a follow up statements:

- "There's a reason that person is in a supervisory position, and I know I'd learn something from them, no matter how old they are. I'd look forward to their perspective."
- "Age doesn't matter to me at all. What matters in a great boss is leadership ability, and knowledge of the business as well as future trends, enthusiasm, and communication skills."
- "I usually find that if someone knows a little less than me because they're younger or don't have as much experience, they know more than me in another area. I learn new things from just about everyone and I enjoy it."

How do you make decisions?

With this question, the interviewer's looking to see what your decision-making process is like. How do you think? How do you approach a problem? Can you think critically about it and come to a rational, data-based solution or decision?

You can walk them through the process of how you go about making a decision—talk about how you gather information, how you learn more about the problem, who you talk to, what books you read, what resources you consult, and what factors you take into account when you decide.

A great way to answer this is to walk them through a difficult decision you made (with a successful outcome).

Maybe it's how you made the decision to **fire** someone, or it's how you made the decision to **assign resources** to a particular function, even though it was unpopular.

Tell your story using a **STAR** format:

- **Situation or Task** –

  Talk about what you were faced with. What was going on? Why was this a problem? What goal were you not hitting that you needed to hit?

- **Action** –

  What did you do? Who did you talk to? What did you read? How did you take in information? Did you try any preliminary solutions before you settled on the final one?

- **Result** –

  Reinforce that you made the right decision by talking about the positive outcome that happened because of your decision. Maybe your decision on resources made a ton of money for the company, or maybe it set you up to develop a new market where you hadn't been before, or maybe it just got one new customer that has turned into a loyal and profitable long-term relationship.

Let the interviewer know that you have no problem making sound, reasoned decisions, because it's part of your job. Walk them through how you think so they can be comfortable with letting you make decisions for them in their role.

How do you take advantage of your strengths?

Asking about your strengths is just as common as asking about your weaknesses. Essentially, this is "why should we hire you?" This is a great opening to **highlight your best-fit qualities** for the job.

The job search is, at its core, a sales process. The employer is like a buyer, or customer, looking for the perfect product to will solve a problem or provide a solution. You are the product that's up for 'sale.' But there's no salesman waiting to sing your praises to this hiring manager—that's your task.

Think about what quality, characteristic or skill you have that will help you do this job especially well. Where will you shine? Don't be afraid to brag...that's essentially the point of this question. And don't be too generic: "I'm driven to succeed, so I work harder than everyone else."

They want to know what YOU can do for the organization, so they can decide whether or not to hire you.

Come up with a few **strengths** that you can **quantify** in some way, because the question is 'how do you take advantage of your strengths', and **the point of every job is to make money or save money or time (which is money) for the company**.

You take advantage of your strengths when you use them to accomplish those money-making or money-saving things for the company.

Have some kind of story or example that illustrates or demonstrates how you've used this strength. For instance:

****

"I am a great listener, and that has helped me build especially strong relationships with my customers. My accounts stay with me X times longer than average because of this."

(Or, your listener skill could help you get projects done faster/ more accurately because you pay attention to the nuances/ details/ whatever. Say what benefits come from this, and quantify them.)

****

"I am very detail-oriented, so I am an organizational powerhouse. In my last position, I was able to successfully maintain X% more accounts than everyone else, making me the top performer."

****

"I am comfortable talking to everyone, which makes me especially successful at going after new business. In my last role, I brought in X new customers in 6 months, that were worth about $X."

****

"I have a lot of experience in X, which means that I can hit the ground running for you and start achieving the X, Y, and Z you would like to see immediately."

****

Think about yourself and what YOUR strengths really are. That's the way to make yourself stand out. No one else is going to have your **unique set of strengths, skills, talents, personality traits, education, or training**.

Make sure that the ones you point out are relevant to this position, so the employer will care about them. If you need to, comb through the job description and think about why you'd be good at X or Y that they have listed.

Whatever you say, be able to **point out the benefit to the employer**—either with **something you've done in the past** (with quantification, if you can) or with **something you will be able to do** for them.

Don't be afraid to brag on yourself. They want to hear how fantastic you are, **they want to hear why they should hire you** over someone else, and they won't know unless you tell them.

Key to a Great Interview – Quantification

Describe your achievements in terms of numbers, dollars, or percentages that answer the hiring manager's (interviewer's) primary question: "How can this person benefit MY company?"

How does this position compare with others you're applying for?

The question behind this question is,
"Why do you want THIS job, with THIS company?"

They want to know that you are truly interested in this job, or if this one is your 'safety net' in case the one you really want doesn't work out. They're also probing to see if you are applying anywhere else, and trying to get a handle on what it would take to get you. The good news is that if they ask this, they are interested in you.

Don't say, "This is the only one I'm applying for," even if it is.

Is this your only interview?

I hope not...in a job search, it's extremely rare for one interview to result in a job.

Plus, some of the best jobs available are part of the over 70% found in the 'hidden job market'.

Find the best jobs and get multiple interviews so you have the CHOICE about which job to take...that is an amazing feeling.

Get my Hidden Jobs Finder today at http://CareerConfidential.com.

You want them to think that someone else wants you. At the same time, don't overdo it. Letting them think that you've applied all over the place, to anyone who'll have you, is not the way to make yourself seem like a desirable candidate—it just makes you seem desperate for a job, any job.

A great way to handle this question is to breeze past the outright comparison and point out what especially attracts you to this company and this opportunity, following up with why you're a good fit for it:

"It's very competitive. I am talking with a couple of other companies, but what I especially like about this one is X, Y, and Z. I believe it is an especially good fit for me because of A, B, and C."

(Don't give them the idea that you are talking to *a lot* of other companies, because it makes you seem more interested in collecting a paycheck from anyone willing to sign it rather than someone who is truly interested in the work and finding the right fit.)

You could follow up this statement in a couple of ways:

1) "Do you agree with me so far?"

This is a great time to **ask if they agree that you seem like a good fit**, or some other question that puts the ball back in their court so that you can see what they might be thinking about you.

2) "How do I compare to the other candidates you're interviewing?"

They're asking what you think about how it's going, so turn it around and ask them how they think it's going.

*** If a recruiter has contacted you about this job, this is the only time it's OK to say, "I am not applying anywhere else. I am happy where I am, but when Recruiter Smith called, it seemed like an exciting opportunity that I wanted to explore a little further." In this case, the employer will realize that they are going to have to sweeten the pot to lure you away from your current employer (where you're very happy).

How does your previous experience relate to this position?

This is a GREAT question if you can get it. It's another version of, "Why should we hire you?" You have the power here to **highlight your best qualities**. They want to know **why you're a good fit for the job**, and  are looking for information that will make their decision an easy one.

If you DO have related experience, this is easy. Just summarize it, pointing out a few pertinent details along the way. If you've already asked, "What does your ideal candidate look like?" then you know what's most important to them, and you can mention relevant things from your own background. If you haven't asked about their ideal candidate, then you can base your answer from what you read in their job description.

But remember: every candidate can explain a direct relationship. **To stand out, add examples with _quantification_ to your answer where you can.** For example, if your experience is in retail and this job is in retail, you have plenty of experience. Where you **stand out** is when you also tell them that you boosted sales by **30%** or you won the company customer service award **3 years** in a row or you reduced turnover by **50%** by implementing X program.

Key to a Great Interview - Quantification

Describe your achievements in terms of **numbers, dollars, or percentages that answer the hiring manager's (interviewer's) primary question:** "How can this person benefit MY company?"

If you are a new graduate or if you are switching careers, your experience may not clearly show why you'd be a good fit for the job, so your job is to **connect those dots** for them and explain **how your skills are transferable** to this position. Things you'll typically want to point out are:

- communication skills
- organization
- project management
- time management

- problem-solving
- multitasking
- professional contacts

Think about what it is that you have that would make you successful in this job.

In this case, you also want to show that **you can learn new things quickly** by giving them an example of a time that you did: "My job was X, but Y situation came up and they asked me to handle it. Here's how I did it." Walk them through your thought process to show them your **strategic thinking** and **ability to adapt**, both of which are tremendously beneficial in a new role.

Key to a Great Interview!

If they ask you about your experience, they are trying to see you in the role. The best way to help a hiring manager see you in the role is to show them your 30-60-90-Day Plan.

Say, "My experience relates through X, Y, and Z. But to really show you how I could step into THIS role and be successful, I've created a 90-day plan for how I would approach this job with my skills and even fill in the gap that I have in X. Can we take a few minutes to walk through it?"

The interviewer will be curious to see your plan, and happy to see such a substantial answer to this question. They'll be able to see you in the role much more clearly, which puts them further along the road to offering you the job.

Find out more about 30-60-90-Day plans at http://CareerConfidential.com

How have you handled difficult situations with employees?

Every hiring manager has had a difficult situation with an employee. With this question, the interviewer is mostly looking for **how you respond to underperformance**, which is the most common difficult situation. A manager who can turn around an underperformer is a **highly valued** piece of any organization.

Think about a time when you had to deal with a problem employee and had a **positive outcome.**

Use the **STAR** format:

- **S**ituation or **T**ask
- **A**ction
- **R**esult

Situation or Task

Tell them what was going on with this employee. What was happening? What was the behavior? How long had it been going on? How was it affecting the bigger picture?

Action

Walk them through what you did to address the problem. How did you intervene? Did you have a talk with the employee? Did you set up a Personal Improvement Plan? What was involved in the plan? Was it a simple plan, or a multi-step one? Did that solve it, or did you have to meet with the employee again? Did you have to get anyone else involved? Did you ask anyone for advice? Did you use any resources? What was the employee's reaction to your intervention? Walk them through the action you took so they can see your thought process.

Result

What happened as a result of your actions? Did the employee have a better attitude or increased performance? Maybe you found a better-fitting position within the company for the employee where they are now successful.

Use quantification wherever you can. Did this happen in 2 weeks or 6 months? Did the employee's performance improve by 5% or 80%? Did you save money by not having to train a new employee?

Walk them through a good example with a positive outcome so they can see how you approach a difficult situation like this, how you think, and if your goals line up with them as a company.

How many tennis balls can you fit into a limousine?

Will you get asked a brainteaser question in your interview? Maybe, maybe not.

Yes, they can seem ridiculous. The method behind the madness is to evaluate how you think and how you approach a problem. The key is to be ready for anything, and don't get flustered.

If they ask you any kind of **brainteaser question**:

- How many tennis balls in a limousine?
- How would you move Mount Fuji?
- How many gas stations are there in the US?

Just remember that you don't have to get the exact right answer. What you need to do is demonstrate that:

A) **You don't get flustered, confused, or thrown off your game** by the unexpected.
B) You can come up with a **reasoned, logical approach to problem solving.**

So just take a deep breath and **start thinking through the question out loud**. If you need a pen and paper to help you think (I would), then use the ones you brought with you to take notes.

For tennis balls in a limousine, maybe I would say, "I would first have to look up the average cubic feet of the inside of a limo, and then I would do a simple calculation based on that number divided by the size of a tennis ball. Or, I could get a 1 foot cube, fill it with tennis balls, count those, and multiply that by the average cubic square feet of the inside of a limo." So now, I've shown them that I can come up with **multiple ways to approach and solve a problem on the fly**.

If I were asked to move Mount Fuji, I might say, "How far? I need some parameters." (*It's OK to ask questions to clarify or get more information.*) Or I might use humor: "A bulldozer load at a time." Or, if I wanted to be creative, I might say, "I'd have a contest for anyone who could move the biggest bucketful of Mount Fuji 1 mile, and the winner would get a prize."

HINT!

Take paper and pen to your job interviews!

Use it to sketch out ideas to help yourself think and better answer interview questions.

Take notes for your thank you note and second interview.

If I were asked "How many gas stations are there in the U.S?" I'd probably estimate how many gas stations there might be in a small town of say, 10,000 people and start multiplying until I got to the approximately 300 million people there are in the U.S.

In these kinds of questions, **the answer is not the point as much as is the process of getting there.**

How will you identify problems and opportunities on the job?

This is a great question that allows you to vividly demonstrate your **creativity, critical thinking,** and **problem-solving skills**.

They want you to walk them through **the process you use to identify top issues and opportunities to move the company forward.** You have several ways to address this question:

(1) You can answer by giving them an **example** of something you identified in the past and what actions you took to either address it or take advantage of it, and what the results were. This approach is something you can use **if you have a strong, quantified example of something that had a major impact on your company** (such as an innovative new marketing program, an efficiency-boosting scheduling change, or something that *significantly* saved or made the company money).

Tell your story using a **STAR** format:

- **S**ituation or **T**ask (Set up the story—what happened? What was your goal?)
- **A**ction (What did you choose to do and why?)
- **R**esult (What happened as a result of your actions? Quantify this wherever possible.)

(2) This is a good time to talk about the **80/20 Rule**, and how you use it to determine where you're going to get the most impact from your actions. This is a very important guiding principle that applies to productivity in every area of your life. It is a data-based decision-making process.

80/20 Rule

A long, LONG time ago, an Italian economist named Pareto noticed that 80% of the wealth in Italy was held by 20% of the people. Joseph Juran took Pareto's Principle and successfully applied it to quality management--and the 80/20 Rule was born.

The 80/20 Rule says (among other things) that 80% of sales come from 20% of customers, or that **80% of your results come from 20% of your effort.**

It's about **productivity** and identifying the **significant tasks/actions** that contribute most to it. Prioritize the most important tasks, and you become **super-efficient and effective.** You will spend time on the things that matter.

---

(3) This is an ideal time to introduce your **30-60-90-Day Plan**: "I'm so glad you asked that, Mr. Manager. I've worked up an outline of how I would approach the job in the first 90 days, and it includes how I intend to go about identifying areas where I can make the most impact in terms of solving your problems and implementing actions to help us grow." And then get out your plan and start going over it with the hiring manager.

Key to a Great Interview!

Introducing your 30-60-90-day plan is an excellent answer to a forward-thinking question like this one. They want to know what life is going to look like with you on the job and how they can expect you to **tackle problems, identify opportunities, and contribute to the growth of the company**. The 90-day plan demonstrates how you'll hit the ground running to do just that.

Find out more about 30-60-90-Day Plans at http://CareerConfidential.com.

How would people you have worked with describe you?

This is an important question, for two reasons:

1) This is actually going to be **how you describe yourself**.

What you say should be very **positive**: "They would say that I am a hard worker, who is very thoughtful and strategic about the work that I do, that I am proud of my work and what I've accomplished. They would say that I never want to let anyone down, and that I always want to exceed the expectations of the people I am working for. And they would say that I am someone they can trust, rely on, and call on when they are having issues, that I am someone who goes above and beyond."

Whatever you say, **be prepared to give examples** that illustrate what you just said. If you say that you are someone who goes above and beyond, you need to have an example of a time that you did that. If you don't have an example, you will be in trouble.

2) What you say needs to be **close to what your references will say** about you, because they will ask.

If what you predict is miles away from what they actually say about you, you'll seem very out of touch with how you're perceived by others, which doesn't say good things for your communication skills. (Always know what your references will say about you.)

This is a great time to thumb over to the section in your **brag book** where you've printed out **emails or notes from bosses, colleagues, or clients to actually show them what others have said about you**. If there are especially positive comments in your **performance reviews, or any awards letters,** those would be good to show, also.

 Key to a Great Interview!

Your Brag Book is a "wow" factor in your interview. If you haven't already, start putting yours together today. You will be amazed at how much it helps your interview performance.

If you'd like more info for how to put yours together, check out **Career Confidential's Brag Book eReport on Amazon**

How would you guide an alien through making a peanut butter sandwich?

This seems like a silly question, but it actually gets right to the heart of how you **think and communicate**.

How well can you teach someone else?

Can you step back from something as completely basic as a peanut butter sandwich and remember to **explain the steps** to someone who knows absolutely nothing?

Can you **put yourself in their shoes**?

Are you a good **communicator**?

So I would say,

"First of all, we have to assume nothing. So there's an alien sitting at the table. Does he know he's hungry, or do we have to explain that, as well? Here on Earth, when we are hungry, we have to physically eat food or drink, something that has calories in it, or we have a big problem. Then I would show him what peanut butter looks like, and what bread looks like, and what a knife looks like.

I would show him how to twist the lid on the jar of peanut butter to the right to open it, and let him practice. Then I would show him how to open the package of bread and get two slices, and lay them side-by-side on the table. I would demonstrate how to hold the knife, and let him have it. Then I would tell him to dip the knife in the peanut butter and draw it out.

Then I would tell him to apply the peanut butter to one side of a piece of bread, and spread it around. Then I would tell him to place the other piece of bread on top of that one, so that the peanut butter is in the interior of the sandwich. That's how I would guide an alien through making a peanut butter sandwich."

You want to **talk about everything and assume nothing.** They are looking to see how you communicate.

When you are training people at work, you have to make sure you **stop and explain everything**, even if you think it's self-explanatory. There's no telling what your trainee might be bringing to this process in terms of past experience, so you need to make sure there are no misunderstandings.

I see you had an internship. Did you pursue a full-time job with them? What happened?

Internships are fantastic opportunities, and if you've had one, that puts you ahead of someone who didn't.

Very often when someone has an internship, it turns into a full-time job for them. So if yours didn't, why not? Did that company have a problem with you? (Which means, will they have a problem with you?)

They are looking for reassurance that there is no risk in hiring you, so what you are trying to do in answering this question is to **eliminate any perceived risks**.

If you did NOT pursue a full time job with them, that's no problem. There are lots of reasons why you might not have, not all of them negative. For now, talk about what a **great relationship** you had, and what a great internship it was. If you can, mention that they could even give a **reference** for you. If they will give you a good reference, the risk of hiring you is gone.

If you DID pursue a full-time job with them, and it didn't work out, make sure the interviewer understands **it wasn't you**; it was them (the company). You could say that they didn't have an opening at the time, or that they cut back on new hires and didn't hire any interns, or that they were in the middle of a layoff and weren't bringing in any new staff. You could say that they didn't have a position open in your area or in your preferred geographical location. **They would have liked to hire you**, but it just didn't work out. Again, if they can give you a good **reference**, that is a complete risk-eliminator.

If you pursued the job with them because they did have open position and you just didn't get it, maybe you could speak about the fact that you didn't have some sort of an experience that now you do have. Something needs to have changed in you or on your part between when they decided they didn't want you and now. **Whatever it was that made you a risk before should be gone**, so that you are not a risk to your new company.

If I were to ask your current boss to tell me one thing you do that drives them crazy, what would they say?

Even though you're spending the whole interview singing your praises, the interviewer knows you're not perfect. They know you've got a wart or two, and want to find it before they hire you—so, they ask about your flaws. The usual question is, "What's your greatest weakness?" but some interviewers get creative and ask this one.

As with the weakness question, **choose a real weakness that does not directly affect your success on this job**—nothing that would have a major impact on your performance.

Things to **stay far, far away from**:

"I ask for too much direction." - This gives the impression that you don't know what you're doing.

"I run late on projects." - A manager can't rely on someone who commits to something and doesn't meet it—over and over again.

"My boss was mad because I didn't tell her about a problem fast enough."

You might feel justified because you were trying to handle it yourself, but this interviewer doesn't want to think you ignore problems until they're causing a major and maybe unfixable issue.

****

Whatever you choose to say, follow it up with some statement indicating that you either are **taking steps to improve**, or that even though it's not necessarily a saint-like quality, it does **help you succeed in your job**.

For instance, my bosses would have told you that I'm very **impatient**. At times, it causes me a problem socially and in my family life. But that same impatience is what drove me to be a top sales rep and helped me climb the ladder to management very quickly.

Maybe your **desk is messy** and your boss is a neat freak. Unless you are directly dealing with clients or lose things, it shouldn't be a problem. This is a case where it might drive your boss crazy personally, but it doesn't affect your work.

Maybe you get so involved in your work you **lose track of time** and you've been late to a few internal meetings (not great, but not the worst reason to be late). That's something your boss can't stand, so you started setting **an alarm on your phone** and you haven't been late since.

Don't choose a clichéd answer, like you're a perfectionist or you work too hard, but choose something completely insignificant to your success in this job.

The one exception to this would be if you were actually fired for cause. They will be talking to your former boss. This is your chance to soften the story, present your side, and tell why whatever got you fired is never, ever going to be a problem again.

If I were to ask your current boss what your greatest strength is, what would they say?

If you had to choose only one quality to explain why they need to hire you, and your entire interview was limited to talking about that one quality, which one would you choose? That's the one to mention in this answer.

I might try to stack the deck and include a few more in my answer anyway: "My boss would have a hard time choosing between my people skills, my work ethic, or X."

"X" would depend on your individual situation and the job description. It could be:

- "My ability to take steps out of almost any process and make it more efficient."

- "My ability to see the big picture and set smart strategies."

- "My meticulous attention to detail."

- "My ability to take the lead on almost any team project and get everyone working together."

- "My ability to fit into almost any team, get along with everyone, and accomplish our goal."

- "My creativity, combined with my business sense."

- "My knack for finishing projects on time and under budget every time."

- "My nose for finding new opportunities to generate revenue."

Whatever you say, **follow it up with a story** that tells about a time you did this, to give an example: "Recently, I did X and my boss was so thrilled that she mentioned me to the VP and I got a mention in the monthly meeting as an example to follow." This is going to help them **visualize** you in action on the job and get comfortable with the idea of working with you.

Always try to **quantify your answer**. Provide **numbers, dollars, or percentages** to describe what happened, what action you took, or what the outcome was. Let's say you said your greatest strength was your nose for finding new opportunities to generate revenue: "Last year, I realized that our product would be perfect for X market, and we hadn't ventured there yet. So I told my boss and together we came up with a plan that ended up generating $X in sales in the first 6 months."

Whatever your example is, tell a story that provides this quantification for your interviewer. This is powerful **evidence** that you can do what you say you can do, and you understand that your role in this company (and any role in any company) is to make **measurable progress** or provide **measurable results** that help them grow **financially**.

If you are employed, how are you managing time to interview?

Why would they ask you this question? It's because they are trying to find out if you are lying to or 'cheating on' your current employer. Are you **honest**? Do they know you're looking? Are you a sneak? Did you tell them you were sick? (I hope not.)

Always **answer this question briefly**:

"I am taking personal time to do this today."

If there is a need for you to elaborate, you can say: "I am selective about where I interview, because I only want to consider jobs that would be a perfect fit, so it's not taking much time away from work."

If you could choose any company to work for, which one would it be?

This is a question of **fit**. Will you fit within this organization?

With this question, they are looking to see **how you think**, and if you have **thoughtfully considered** where you want to work, and **what kind of environment** you want to be in. It's a way for them to understand your **character** and your **thought process**. Are you in this for your career, or for just a paycheck?

Ideally, you want to **describe a company with characteristics similar to the one you're interviewing with,** and talk about the characteristics of this company that are most **appealing** to you. Talk about how you are looking for a company that has growth opportunities, that has the same values and ethics that you have, or that will use your skill sets (whether yours are in Accounting or Sales or Operations or whatever). **Help them see how their company is a good fit for you.**

Maybe the company you want to work for is simply in a **specific industry** (medical, beverages, transportation, information technology). Are you looking for a **small company or a large one**? A **public or private** company? **Profit or non-profit**? **Government or private-sector**?

Say what it is about it that appeals to you: "I want to work for a small company because small companies generally tend to be more fluid, more innovative, and more growth-oriented, and I think that's exciting."

Stay away from saying anything bad about your previous companies: "As long as a company doesn't do X (whatever X was that was so awful), then I'll be thrilled." That's a very negative statement that indicates you are running AWAY from somewhere, rather than running TO somewhere. If you are running away, it doesn't matter so much where you end up. If you are running TO somewhere, it does. You have a goal. It's a positive thing.

 Always Remember: Under no circumstances do you name a specific company that is not this one—even as a joke.

If this is your ideal company, by all means, say so (and tell them why) and let your natural enthusiasm shine through. That's a very appealing quality in someone interviewing for a job.

If you get the job, how could you lose or make money for me?

This question really gets at, "Do you understand the job and what it takes to be successful?"

You might be tempted to say, "There's no way I could lose money for you!" But the truth is that everyone can make mistakes, and it's good to show that you recognize where those pitfalls are and that you know how to avoid them.

You could say, "In this position, someone could lose money by making a mistake in X, Y, or Z."

Follow this up with, "I could make money for you first by avoiding those mistakes, and then by being successful at A, B, and C."

"A, B, and C" should be those tasks or actions that are **central to your success in this job**.

Every position in every company has an impact on the company's financial success—even the janitor, because that's the person who keeps the facility clean and attractive. The facility's attractiveness helps to make it a pleasant place to work, so that top performers in the field enjoy working there. Cleanliness helps keep accidents down, so the company isn't paying out in worker's comp. And, it sets the company in the customer's or client's mind as not only a nice place to do business, but reassures them that this company takes care of details as well as the big picture.

Give an example (**quantified**, if you can) to illustrate how you can make money: "I did this at my last job, where I created XYZ that was responsible for pushing us over the top on our performance goals for the year by 30%."

Once you answer the question, this is an **excellent** place to bring up your **30-60-90-Day Plan:**

"I've thought a lot about how I could make money for you and be successful at this job. I worked up an outline of what I would do in the first 90 days to really hit the ground running. Would you like to see my ideas?"

Any good interviewer or hiring manager is going to be intensely curious about you and your plan you've put together. This will give them much more information about you and how you think so they can make a good decision about whether or not to offer you the job. As you go through the plan, you'll be **discussing ways you can make money for the company** and getting this hiring manager's input on how you can be super-successful in this role.

 Key to a Great Interview!

A 30-60-90-day plan helps make it
an easy decision to hire you!

**Find out more about 30-60-90-Day Plans at
http://CareerConfidential.com**

If you knew things at your company were rocky, why didn't you get out sooner?

LOYALTY

You may get asked this question if you were laid off in a massive restructuring, downsizing, or other shakeup, and you need to have a good answer.

This is a good place to **underscore your loyalty** to the company you work for:

"I was so focused on doing my job well and taking up the slack where others had left or been laid off that I just didn't have the time to look around for another job. I was hoping that it would turn around, because that was a great company, and a great place to work for many years."

You would **never** want to answer this question by giving the idea that you were clueless ("I didn't know it was as rocky as it turned out to be") or helpless ("I tried to look for something else, but no one else was hiring"). Both of those kinds of answers make you seem weak and less-than-desirable as a new hire.

Always answer questions like these in a **positive way** that shows that it was **your choice**, that you stayed out of loyalty, and that you fought until the bitter end.

If you were at a business lunch and you ordered a rare steak and they brought it to you well-done, what would you do?

This is not just a question of dining etiquette, it's also a question about **how you respond to mistakes or problems** and how concerned you are with the comfort of your clients or customers.

"Mistakes happen. I would be disappointed, but because that's simply a preference of mine, it would not be worth making the other person feel uncomfortable eating without me or having to wait until my food came back. So, if it isn't going to give me food poisoning, I would just eat it."

If you were running a company that produces X and the market was tanking for that product, what would you do?

This question probes for how you think—are you **strategic**? How do you **approach problems** and come up with **solutions**?

This is like any other behavioral interview question, only it's more realistic than "If an airplane landed in the parking lot, what would you do?"

In this case, you are pretending to run the company.

A good CEO:

- thinks through problems
- gathers and develops resources
- looks at the data
- makes thoughtful, strategic decisions
- works to position her company to succeed now and in the future

So a good answer might be:

"I would look at why the market was tanking—is it a temporary situation or does it look permanent? Is it the economy? Is it a change in social trends? I might try to conduct a survey of my customers to see what they're thinking. Based on all the information I gathered, I would look at my product to see if it could be improved or modified to fit the new paradigm, or if maybe it just needed to be marketed with a fresh approach. In addition, I would look at other potential markets for my product that we hadn't yet explored."

If you have questions, ask them.

It's perfectly acceptable to **gather more information** before you decide on a plan of action. Walk them through your thought process. **Help them see your problem-solving approach and solution-producing abilities.**

If you were the CEO of this company, what are the top 2 things you would do?

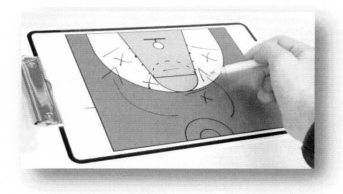

This is another situational interview question, or behavioral interview question, that delves into not just how you think and how you approach problems, but also into how well you've prepared for this interview.

- How well do you know this company?
- Have you done your homework?
- Do your goals and thinking line up with theirs?

They won't want to hear that you would come in with big, sweeping changes to radically transform everything—for one, that's threatening, and two, if you thought the company was that off-track, why would you want to work there?

They also don't want to hear that everything is great and you would change or improve nothing—if that were so, they why would they need you?

If you've done your homework and looked the company up in terms of:

- **news releases**
- **LinkedIn** pages or discussions
- **Facebook** pages
- contacting **current or previous employees**

Then, you'd have some idea of the direction the company is going, and you could contribute an idea or comment to that.

If this question comes after some discussion already in the interview, you could work that into your answer:

"**Based on our discussion** about X, I think that a good direction would be to look into Y—depending on how A, B, and C factor into it."

Anything you suggest needs to have some **financial benefit** for the company. I'd **stay away from** talking about implementing 'feel-good' initiatives like flextime or a company health club and focus instead on things that relate to the primary objective of the company.

Maybe you don't have anything concrete to contribute. In that case, you could talk about **how you would approach a problem** like that:

"First, I would make sure I knew everything I needed to know about what is currently going on, I'd talk to people in the company, I'd see what the projections are for the next year, and then I'd start evaluating different plans of action, based on that data."

Then, here's the **killer follow up** to that statement:

"But that's more theoretical. If you'd like to know how I would approach a new role in the here and now, I have put together a 90 day plan for what I would do in the first 3 months in this job. As we go through it together, you'll see my thought process and learn a lot more about me. Would you like to see it?"

The discussion of your first 90 days in this job will have a much bigger impact on how they see you and your success in this role than the answer to this theoretical question.

 Key to a Great Interview!

A 30-60-90-Day Plan is a sure-fire way
to show how:

- You think strategically
- You could step into the role and be successful immediately

This plan makes it an easy decision for them to hire you.

Find out more about 30-60-90-Day Plans at http://CareerConfidential.com

If you won the lottery, would you still work?

Asking this personality interview question is a way for the interviewer to try to establish rapport and get to know the 'real' you. It's also a vehicle they try to use to determine your work ethic, and whether you do this work because you're sincerely enthusiastic about the job, or because it pays for your food, shelter, and hobbies.

There are 3 viable ways you could answer this question:

  (1) "**I don't know.** It's easy to guess as to what we would do in an extraordinary situation like that, but it's very hard to actually know. If I told you I'd keep working, you might not believe me, but I truly enjoy what I do

and get a lot of personal satisfaction in a job well done. It would be hard to walk away from that feeling of getting up every morning and feeling challenged by my day and successful at the end of it."

This answer at least lets them know that **you care about your job** and you enjoy being successful at it, for reasons other than money.

(2) "We all have fantasies of relaxing on the beach, but I am someone who likes to keep growing, learning, and accomplishing. So if I didn't work anymore, I would at least explore some of the **things I've always wanted to do**, like travel or learn how to do X. I certainly wouldn't run out of ideas for new things to do!"

This answer shows that you are someone who is **energetic, curious, and constantly growing**—all great qualities.

(3) You could answer this one with **humor** and a big smile on my face (one of my favorite tactics): "I don't know if I'd still work, but I'd definitely buy everyone I knew a car to celebrate. Would I know you by then because of our long and successful working relationship?"

This answer ought to make them laugh and relax with you, which is always a good thing in an interview.

Is it more important to be lucky or skillful?

This question is an **attitude** question. How you answer it will tell the interviewer a lot about **how you look at the world**. Are you an optimist or a pessimist? Do you consider yourself someone with good things going on in their life, or bad things?

It's important to **be positive** in your answer.

You never want to sound like, "Well, it must be more important to be lucky, because those are the people who catch all the breaks!" This shows them that you consider yourself unlucky and are more than a little resentful of that.

My personal answer is:

"I think that if you're skillful, then you create your own luck. You get to be skillful by putting yourself out there, developing those skills, and when you do that, opportunities show up. When you are prepared for those opportunities with what you need to take advantage of them, that's what most people call 'luck.'"

Or you could say something else that shows you have a positive attitude and you work hard, such as:

"I think I was very lucky to have been born into a family that valued education and taught me how to work hard. That background led me to develop the skills I need to do this job, which put me in this conversation with you today. So in that sense, I've been both."

If you have some kind of an **issue** in your background, such as a **career setback**, an **illness** or an **illness of a family member** that's kept you out of the workforce for a few years, this might be the time to talk a little more philosophically about luck and skill:

"Well, I've dealt with adversity in the form of X, that I felt made me very unlucky at the time. But I learned A, B, and C from that which is helping me today to be better at Y and Z. So while I wouldn't have wished that on anyone, I think that it's developed more confidence/a better attitude/a more positive outlook that will help me to be stronger than ever before."

Whatever you say, keep your answer positive.

Job Interview Question 49

Is there any question I haven't asked you that I should?

This question makes me want to use humor to answer it. Smile and say, "I think you should ask me 'When can you start?'"

This is a great time to 'close' for the job. If you don't know what closing is, it's a sales technique for sealing the deal. When you close, you are at the 'rubber meets the road' point where they're either in or out, and you need to know which.

If you say, "I think you should ask me when I can start," and they **smile** or otherwise indicate that they are thinking along those same lines, then you know you've done a good job in this interview.

If they start briskly backpedaling, you know they are leaning toward going with someone else, and you should say (with surprise), "Oh, that doesn't sound good. Is there some reason you wouldn't move me forward?" This gets them to **tell you what problem or doubt they do have**, and you might have a chance to address it and resolve it right there, and possibly **save your job offer.**

This is a great opportunity to plug any holes you might have in your discussion about your experience or fit for the job.

If they haven't asked you about something that you know would impress them, now's the time to bring that up. Make this a great story that is **quantified** and **demonstrates your value**. Your story might also be part of your attempt to eliminate their doubts about hiring you.

Tell your story using the **STAR** format:

- **S**ituation or **T**ask (Set up the story—what happened? What was your goal?)
- **A**ction (What did you choose to do and why?)
- **R**esult (What happened as a result of your actions? Quantify this wherever possible.)

Everything I've said so far, though, assumes that you've already gone over your 30-60-90-day plan in your interview. If you have not had a chance to discuss that with the hiring manager, now is the time:

"I think you should ask me how I would approach this job and be successful in my first 3 months, because I've worked up a very nice outline with some great ideas that I'd love to talk over with you and get your take on."

 Key to a Great Interview!

A 30-60-90-day plan helps make it an easy decision to hire you!

Find out more about 30-60-90-Day Plans at http://CareerConfidential.com

---

It's your dime.
(Interviewer doesn't ask questions)

I once had a candidate go to a **sales interview,** sit down and....nothing. The hiring manager just ignored her and played with a pen. That's enough to rattle the most skilled and experienced person.

The **wrong thing to do** would have been to get rattled, and just sit there, too. It wouldn't take long before the manager would have gotten up and invited her to leave—or even walked out without saying anything.

However, this woman was unflappable. She smiled at the 'interviewer' and said, "I'm so happy to meet with you today. I understand that you are in the market for a new sales rep.

What are the most important qualities you're looking for in someone for this job?"

With that question, she got the hiring manager talking, they went on with the interview, and she got the job.

What the hiring manager was looking for was someone who had a strong enough personality and **confidence** to walk into a cold-call situation and **make the sale**. If this woman had shown that she couldn't even step out of her comfort zone to stand up for herself, how would she ever find the strength to stand up for the company's product in the face of an initially disinterested customer?

I've seen a lot of companies "play" with candidates this way—put them in uncomfortable situations to see what they're made of. One company routinely had a cab collect interviewees from the airport and then drop them off at an incorrect location. Another company did something similar—they had the cabbie deliberately take a long and winding route to the interview, making the interviewee late. They learned a lot about their candidates by **seeing how they reacted under pressure,** how they treated the cabbie (who was in full cahoots with them), **and what they did to rectify the situation**.

Never let anything make you lose your composure in an interview situation. Even if you think something is just too weird, it may be a play to rattle you and see what you'll do. Just smile at the attempt, keep your cool, and keep moving toward your goal.

Tell me a suggestion you have made that was implemented.

- Are you just collecting a paycheck, or do you actively try to improve things in your job?
- Are you creative enough or strategic enough to come up with a better way of doing something?
- How have you made a difference at your job?
- Can you identify problems, analyze the situation, and provide a viable solution?

These are the questions in the interviewer's mind as they ask you about your suggestions that have been implemented. Your suggestion doesn't have to be something earth-shattering that changed the direction of the company forever. It can be a simple one—as long as it provided a **useful benefit**. Choose a suggestion to talk about that illustrates something that would be a positive selling point for you in this job.

Tell them about it using **the STAR format:**

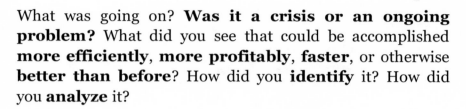

Situation or Task –

What was going on? **Was it a crisis or an ongoing problem?** What did you see that could be accomplished **more efficiently**, **more profitably**, **faster**, or otherwise **better than before**? How did you **identify** it? How did you **analyze** it?

Action –

What was your suggestion? What made you think of it? Were you able to come up with the idea because of your **previous experience**? Did you have to **persuade** your boss, or just mention it and they thought it was a **great idea**?

Result –

What happened as a result of implementing your suggestion? How did the situation **improve**? What got better? How much better? Can you **quantify** what happened (use numbers, dollars, or percentages to describe it)?

Here's an example of a great story using quantification:

A woman wrote a software program code for a call center that **saved them 1.2 seconds every time** they logged in, which in a call center, means millions of times. This 1.2 second time savings added up over the thousands of times they answered the phone every day, and that translated into

savings of millions of dollars for the company over a short amount of time. So when she describes this, she says (using quantification): "I wrote a program code that saved 1.2 seconds for every login, which saved the company $X every year."

 ## Key to a Great Interview!

If you have anything **tangible** that illustrates your story, put it in your **brag book** and point to it while you answer this question. What could this be? The possibilities are many:

- A **brochure** you developed, to show what you can do

- A **note from your boss thanking you** for the suggestion and talking about how it turned out

- **Sales numbers** pre- and post-suggestion

- **Any workplace improvements** pre- and post-suggestion

- A **note from a customer thrilled** with your new system/procedure

- The outline of a **training process you created**

Providing evidence to back up your story or example is a powerful way to stand out from every other candidate.

If you'd like help putting yours together, check out **Career Confidential's Brag Book eReport on Amazon**

Tell me about a time when you helped someone.

It would make the most sense that this question would be asked in service-related jobs, where you've **helped a customer or client**, but it could be asked in relation to other jobs if they want to find out more about your **personality or character**, or whether or not you're **a team player**.

If you are in a service-related job, answer this as **an example of how you work**. Set up the situation, talk about what you did (action) and then tell what happened (result).

A great example to choose is one where the customer or client was unhappy and you turned the situation around.

If you suspect that this is a **personality or character question**, then you can choose almost anything. But be prepared to talk about specifics, and tell the story.

Tell your story using the **STAR** format:

- **S**ituation or **T**ask (Set up the story—what happened? What was your goal?)
- **A**ction (What did you choose to do and why?)
- **R**esult (What happened as a result of your actions? Quantify this wherever possible.)

If you'd like to **highlight that you are a team player**, choose to tell about a time that you helped someone on your team—maybe this would be to finish a project, or maybe this would be helping train them to be better at their job.

If you are in management, you could choose to talk about a time you helped an employee having a hard time—maybe you saved their job and turned them into one of your better performers.

*** **It's best to come up with a *work-related* answer**.

You might hesitate over your answer to this question because it feels like bragging. You have to get past that feeling. They asked you and they are looking for a sincere answer—so give them one.

Tell me about a time when you misjudged a person.

Do not make this story a serious example of how you misjudged them with a severe negative impact. **Keep this story as positive as possible, with the least amount of repercussions.**

My story is this one:

"When I was promoted to Regional Product Manager, my first task was to visit all of my newly-inherited sales reps to evaluate their performance. I flew Southwest out to Orange County, California. I stepped out of the plane to go down the steps to the tarmac (pre-9/11) in my very conservative navy suit with my very conservative background and saw my sales rep waiting for me on the tarmac wearing a pink chiffon scarf waving in the wind 8 feet out behind her.

I thought, 'Oh, no—what am I going to do about this?' I knew that several people had talked about her very positively, and I had had great conversations with her on the phone. It didn't matter. I saw that scarf and made an immediate and negative judgment about her—that she was not a serious sales rep, that she was less competent than what I would want to see, and that she wasn't very business savvy.

As I drove her sales route with her and watched her interact with her customers, I changed my mind. This woman was a fantastic sales rep. She had a warm, friendly style that was very different from my approach, but very effective. She talked to them about their grandkids while she picked up their purchase orders. She was obviously good at her business and was clearly driving business forward. My report was that she was very different, but that she was an outstanding member of the team.

I knew that other sales managers in my company would force this woman to change her style anyway, to fit in with the established company image, but I decided to be open minded and let it go. This woman went on to be one of the top reps in the region."

You could tell the story of how you thought someone at work didn't like you until you realized that this person acted like that toward everyone. You were able to stop taking it personally, and got along just fine with that person with no problems. Since then, you try not to jump to conclusions about other people's motivations before you've gathered more information first.

Tell a brief, innocuous story that taught you a lesson in people skills and made you a better and wiser person today.

Tell me about a time you conveyed technical information to a non-technical audience.

As in any behavioral interview question, **use the STAR format to tell this story**:

Situation – Set up the story. What was going on? What were the circumstances? Why was this important?

In this case, I was with the American Association of Clinical Chemistry, where I was supposed to speak about oncology. There were 400 people in the audience, divided among approximately 75% press people (not technical chemistry or medical people) who wouldn't have the background to understand all the technical jargon, and about 25% extremely technical medical folks who would have been bored and even insulted if I had simplified it too much.

Action – What did you do to address this situation?

I decided to use a PowerPoint presentation to give my talk, with a lot of examples related to their world to illustrate what I was talking about.

Result – How do you know that you were successful? What happened, and can it be quantified in any way?

It was an extremely well-received speech and I was actually graded on it by the folks who put the symposium on and was given a 94% satisfaction with the topic. What they really liked and what they really commented about was my ability to convey extremely technical information to a non-technical audience.

What does this example communicate to the interviewer?

I said what I did, and gave them a **third-party source for the result**. (The symposium leaders said I did great.) The third-party reference is very **powerful**, and the **numbers** that I gave in the 94% satisfaction rate are also very powerful. I could have said that I did well and got great reviews, but that doesn't mean as much as "94% satisfaction."

Even the number that I gave in the beginning, 400 people, is powerful. It provides a **frame of reference** for the story, and is impressive on its own. Some people couldn't give a speech in front of that many people, or would even have the chance to give that speech. If this was your story, and the number was 30 people or 50 people, it would still be powerful with the actual number included.

I've told them about the **situation—what it was and why it was too technical for the audience,** I've told them **what I did to address it,** and I've said **what the result was.** This is a great answer to this question.

Key to a Great Interview - Quantification

Describe your achievements in terms of numbers, dollars, and percentages. See how quantification strengthens your answer:

- "I brought in new clients" or
  "Brought in 20 new clients in 3 months"

- "I delivered product on time and under budget" or
  "98% on-time delivery of product"

- "Maintained accuracy in company database" or
  "100% accuracy in 50,000-item database over 2 years"

**Numbers, dollars, or percentages answer the hiring manager's (interviewer's) primary question:
"How can this person benefit MY company?"**

Tell me about a time you had to take initiative.

Employers want someone who can **take initiative.** Do you have **creativity** to come up with good ideas? Do you have the **decision-making ability** and **good judgment** to take appropriate initiative and the **skill set** to execute on it and be successful?

Use the STAR format:

Situation or Task –

Often in this situation, there would be some sort of **urgency** where there's **no time to discuss** a solution with your boss—but not always. This could be a **nagging problem** or some other situation where you thought, "Hey, I can fix this."

Action –

What plan did you come up with? How did you **think through it**? Did you consider other options? What made you decide to choose the one you did?

Result –

How did the situation **improve or resolve**? Can you **quantify** it?

For instance: "I once had a very angry customer come to me with an unusual problem, X. This wasn't something I had been trained to deal with, but based on our process for handling similar situations, I realized I could offer a new solution for this particular problem without costing the company any money. [Give details about the solution here.] So, the company didn't lose any money, and we kept an important customer, who later came back and ordered another $5000 worth of products."

Or: "I'd been in my job about 3 months when I realized we kept stumbling over the same problem [X]. I mentioned it to my boss, but he was locked into a big project and didn't have time to do anything about it, or even discuss it with me. I talked to some counterparts in other divisions of the company to see what they were doing, realized they had a similar problem with no solution, so I did some online research to get a stronger understanding of what was going on, and found a book related to the topic. I started a discussion about it in a LinkedIn group, and ended up with quite a few helpful insights and ideas.

With that information, I came up with a plan of attack and presented it to my boss, who thought it was terrific and gave me the go ahead. I presented it to my group with a PowerPoint presentation and got them on board. We began implementing it the next day, and it worked like a charm. It improved our X by X% and freed up enough time for us as a whole that we were also able to accomplish XYZ where we'd never had time for that before."

Your answer shouldn't take more than a minute to two at the most. **Walk them through the story, give them the details that help them see your value, and end on a positive note.**

Tell me about a time you planned and coordinated a project from start to finish.

With this question, they want to see your thought process in action—planning, strategic thinking, decision-making, etc. Don't just say, "I once coordinated X and it turned out great." Use the STAR format, walk them through the steps, and include details in your story.

Ideally, you'll choose a work project to talk about, but if you *really* don't have a good example, then use a project from volunteer work of some kind—something where you coordinated something with moving parts or multiple facets, whether that was people, places, or things, and has a successful outcome.

Situation or Task –

What was the project? Why were you doing it? Why were you in charge? What was your goal?

Talk about how you **gathered information** and **used resources** to help you get this done. Did you have to **learn anything new** to complete this project? How did you do that? Did you read a **book**, watch an online **video**, or **talk to someone**?

Talk about the **scope** of the project. **How many people** or groups participated in it? What was the **budget**? What was the **timeline**?

Action –

What did you do? How did you **delegate tasks**? How did you **coordinate** the project? Did you use special **software**? Did you use **Excel spreadsheets**? How did you stay **organized**? Did you encounter any **problems** along the way? How did you decide to address them?

Result –

Did you get the project done **on time**? Did you meet your **goals**? Did you **exceed** your goals? If so, by how much? What did the project **accomplish** for you?

Quantify this as much as you can—maybe you raised $X in a fundraiser, or you came in under budget by 5%, or you completed it X days faster because you took some specific action.

Tell me about a work incident in which you were totally honest, despite a potential risk or downside.

This question explores not only your **honesty**, but also your **courage**, your **judgment**, your **conflict-resolution** skills, your company **loyalty** and whether or not you have the **tact** and **communication** skills to handle delicate situations.

The overriding rules for anything you choose to tell here are:

1) Make sure the downside would have been a negative effect for YOU, not your boss or the company.
2) Make sure the benefit gained would be for the COMPANY or your boss, not you.

This situation could be anything:

- You were the only "Negative Nelly" in the group on a project that everyone was enthusiastic about, because you saw the downside that no one else did—and ended up coming up with a better solution that avoided an expensive mistake.

- You stood up against the group who wanted to hire a particular person, and later found out that the person had caused major trouble in their last job.
- You unintentionally caused a problem that you brought to your boss immediately because you knew you couldn't fix it alone, despite the fact that it was going to make you look bad. You did this because you know that it's more important to take action to correct a problem sooner rather than later, when it could become a much bigger issue.

Use the STAR format:

Situation or Task –

What was the problem you faced? What were the choices in front of you? What were the possible negative outcomes or repercussions of this situation? Did you cause it? Why?

Action –

Why did you decide to be totally honest? What did you say? What did you do? How did you handle it? Did you take them aside to discuss it? If this was in a group discussion, did you try to help someone save face? Did you ask questions until they came to their own conclusion? Or did you lay out your thoughts and follow them through?

Result –

What was the reaction to your honesty? What was decided? What happened as a result of that? Did you learn a lesson that affects how you do your job more successfully today?

 Be careful here—if you talk about a problem that you caused, make it a problem that does not directly affect the central responsibilities of the job you are applying for. Learning from a mistake is fantastic, but *causing* a mistake that indicates you are incompetent at your job is not.

Tell me about the last time you were angry or upset at work. What happened?

Emotional stability is a huge factor in your professionalism at work. No employer wants drama. They want to know that you are in charge of yourself and your emotions and that you do not lose control.

That being said, we all get upset or angry. We are all under a lot of pressure at work, stressful things happen, and just because we try to stay in control at all times doesn't mean that others do, and their actions and reactions have a powerful effect on us.

So the question is not IF you get angry at work, it's WHEN you get angry at work. What do you do? How do you handle that? In this question, they are asking for an example.

Your overall response needs to talk about **how you successfully deal with negative emotions** like this:

"In any stressful, negative, or upsetting situation, I take a step back, take a deep breath, and think it through. It never helps to lash out, and I know that my working relationships are going to have to last a long time, so I never want to do anything to damage them out of anger."

So then, your example might be:

"The last time I got angry was when a co-worker got upset and lashed out at me. I was tempted to retaliate but I know it would have just escalated the situation and not accomplished anything. I knew that she and I normally always get along, and that this was unusual behavior. I looked for what might be causing her anger and realized she was completely stressed out because of X project. I offered to help her with a particularly nasty sticking point, and she was glad of the help and ended up apologizing. We still work well together on a regular basis."

Or, "The last time I got angry at work was when I was working on a particularly detailed and important project and kept getting interrupted. I was on a deadline, so every interruption put me that much farther behind. I could feel myself getting angry, so I stepped back, took a deep breath, and thought about what I could do to solve the problem. I let everyone know that I had to have this done by 2pm so I was shutting my door and turning off my phone until that time. After that, I would be available. I got my project done on time."

Tell me about the toughest negotiation you've ever been in.

This is a common interview question for anyone in a position to buy or sell for their company.

When you answer this question, think about what skills you are highlighting about yourself in your answer. You want to try and focus on your understanding of **basic** and **advanced negotiation techniques** along with higher-level skills, such as **influencing** and **persuading**. You want the end of your negotiation story (and really, any negotiation you enter) to be a **positive** one for everyone.

So, the story you want to tell does not need to be the story of how you simply dug your heels in until they gave up. Persistence is good, but you haven't shown any of those higher-level skills that demonstrate your skill at negotiating.

Use the STAR format:

Situation or Task –

What was going on? Did you need a great deal on material? Did your supplier come to you with an unexpected delay or price increase because they thought they had you all sewn up? Did your company run into a problem that made your supplier or vendor come back demanding a new agreement? Did you have an important but tough customer demanding things you couldn't deliver and keep any sort of a profit?

Action –

What did you do? Did you stall, or come up with an alternative agreement? Did you say you were about to go with someone else? Did you say that at that price, you would be better off producing this in-house? How did you persuade them? What did you bring into the conversation? Did you have to bluff? Did you use any particular negotiating technique? Did you ask questions? What new benefits did you offer? What concessions did you offer and why?

Result –

What was the final agreement? How did it **benefit** you, and why was the other party happy with it—or at least accepting of it? What did they get out of it?

Quantify as much as possible throughout your story, and make sure you end your story on a **positive** note, with a **win** for your company.

Tell me about the worst boss you've ever had.

It's OK to say, "I've never had a bad boss." That's the safest answer.

It's also OK to mention an example that is **vague and neutral**: "I inherited a boss and it happened that our communication styles were very different. I was still as successful at my job as I had ever been, but because I didn't choose him and he didn't choose me, we never really clicked as well as I had done with other managers."

So what if you had the misfortune to work for a tyrannical, backstabbing, manipulative psycho? Don't mention it. **No interviewer wants to hear you talk badly about previous bosses**. It reflects negatively on you and plants the seed in their mind that you are a complainer who won't be happy there, either, and will end up badmouthing them when you leave.

Tell me about your current (most recent) employer (i.e. what do they do, how long they've been in business, etc.).

This question is looking to see how well you know the company you work for (and if you might also learn as much about them). It's a nice vehicle for talking about **how the company fits into the bigger industry** and who all the players are to  demonstrate your **higher-level understanding of the arena**. How you choose to answer it also shows how **detail-oriented** you are and if you can **summarize** effectively.

For instance, a **bad answer** would be: "We are a marketing firm."

A much better answer would be: "ABC Marketing firm is a large regional company focused in the Southwest that's been in business for X years. We handle multi-media campaigns for a wide variety of businesses, from tech corporations, educational institutions, and food companies. Our major competitor is XYZ. They are a similar company, but the critical difference is X."

Job Interview Question 62

Under what circumstances have you found it acceptable to break confidence?

This question is looking at your **ethics** and **values**. There should be very few circumstances in which you would ever break a confidence.

Your answer should be, "I would only ever break a confidence if the person was doing something illegal or unethical and I couldn't talk them into stopping and correcting the behavior."

Walk me through your career from the start to where it is now.

This is a very common interview question similar to "Tell me about yourself" or "Walk me through your resume." This will most likely be asked in the beginning of your interview.

With this question, they get a good **overview** of you as a candidate, they see where you feel that your **greatest strengths** are, and they see whether or not you'd be a **good cultural fit** in the company. This is your chance to **sum up why you're a great candidate** for this job.

The key is to stay focused on the things that will help explain why you are here right now and **why they want to consider hiring you.** Don't get off track into a story that doesn't help you get to that goal, and **don't bring up any personal information**, because it isn't relevant here and won't get you to your goal, either.

They want to know what you did, how one thing led to another, and **why you made decisions to take certain jobs** (especially if one seems to be outside a typical career path) or why you might have a gap of time where you didn't work. Keep your answer to less than 2 minutes.

Start with your **education**: "I got my degree in X from State University and my first job at Acme Corporation in ABC."

Continue with your **background**, mentioning any **jobs, skills, or accomplishments particularly relevant** for this job. This requires some strategic thinking to identify what parts of your history would be the biggest "selling points" for you in this job.

What things could you point out that would give this hiring manager **another reason to offer you the job**? (And what things might make him or her nervous, so what could you say that would alleviate those doubts?) You might say, "I took some time off to deal with a family matter (or whatever it was), and when that was resolved, I got back to work." Whatever you learned along the way that makes you an especially good fit for this job, be sure to mention it. Point out what it was that made you move from one job to another, showing that you were moving TOWARD something in each job that **added to your growth, skill set, or value** in your field.

Never mention that you left a job because it was horrible, or the boss was a jerk. **Always be positive.** Talk about how you moved toward something, not away from something.

Wrap it up with, "And all that led me here. I believe this job is a fantastic place for me to grow professionally even further, and I know that I could move you forward as well, with my experience in X, Y, and Z."

What are some of your leadership experiences?

Any job where you will be managing others or even leading a team will be very interested in previous leadership experiences. They want to know:

- **what kind of leader** you are
- how you **motivate** others
- how you **manage the details**—as well as the people.

If you already have some experience managing others or leading a team, that's great. If you do not already have management experience, that's OK. Think of any time when you organized a project or were placed in charge of getting something done, either at work, at school, or in a volunteer setting.

Use the STAR format to talk about these experiences:

Situation or Task – Were you **placed in charge** of a project? Did you **volunteer** to spearhead a project from start to finish? What was the **scope** of the project? **How many people** did you lead (**quantification**)? What was your **goal**?

Action – How did you start? **How did you decide** who should do what? How did you **communicate** with your team? Did you have to **train** anyone? If this was a volunteer experience, it can be an even stronger example of your leadership ability, because no one was compelled to follow your leadership. What **obstacles** did you face, and how did you **resolve** them?

Result – Tell them about the **successful outcome** of your project. Did you get it done **on time or early**? Did you **reach your goal**? Did you **exceed your goal**? By how much?

Be brief, since you will be talking about multiple experiences, add details, quantify what you can, and be positive and tell stories with a successful outcome.

 Key to a Great Interview - Quantification

Describe your achievements in **numbers, dollars, or percentages** and answer the hiring manager's primary question:
"How can this person benefit MY company?"

What are the most important qualities of successful people? How do you rate yourself in those areas?

For an overall strategy: I would **choose 5 qualities** and rate myself very good on 2-3 and good with room for improvement on the rest.

I would never say that I was outstanding in all 5 areas, because that means that you don't believe you have room to learn and grow, and I believe we all do.

Here are some qualities you could choose:

Dedication –

To be successful, you must want it and be willing to work at it even when it is difficult and you'd rather be doing something else.

Persistence –

It takes self-discipline to be persistent in the face of adversity, but we will always face adversity. The only way to get past it to success is to never give up.

Positive Attitude –

A positive attitude contributes to your success in a thousand ways — in interactions with others, your ability to keep going in the face of obstacles, in your physical health so that you can keep going, and in your expectations. If you can **visualize and expect success**, you are more likely to experience it**.**

Willingness to Listen to Others and Learn –

You can **never stop learning and growing** if you want to be successful. You can learn a lot by reading, and by talking with and listening to others who have also been successful.

A Desire to be a Subject Matter Expert –

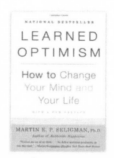
To be successful, you need to **know what you're doing**. You should always be moving toward a being a SME in your field—by reading, listening, and learning.

They Choose Good Mentors –

I have always kept a group of 5 people who know more than me in various areas that I take the time to go have lunch or coffee with on a regular basis. Their advice has absolutely made me **more successful than I would have been without it**.

They Build and Maintain Good Networks –

Your network is there for you when you need to know something, when you need a new job, when you need a new connection. I always recommend that you reach out to contact everyone in your network with a quick email or phone call every 3-6 months, just to say Hi or give them something useful, to maintain that connection.

They Manage Their Emotions –

One of the worst things you can do in a professional setting is lose your temper or cry, no matter what the provocation might be. Successful people practice **self-control**.

They Are Results-Oriented, Not Action-Oriented –

You can do a lot of things and not make any progress or see any results from them. It's never about how hard you work, it's about your results. What works? Successful people plan their next move based on what works and are known not so much for working hard as for getting the job done.

As in all your job interview answers, **be strategic**. Even if you have all of these qualities in abundance, which ones will have **the most impact on your success in THIS job**? Choose those to talk about and point out to your interviewer.

What are your long-term career goals?

The best answer to this really does depend on the company you're interviewing with—is it a flat company or a structured company? Some companies want you to be planning ahead, and others don't have anywhere for you to go—so they will be threatened if you aggressively talk about advancement, promotions, etc.

Either way, don't give the impression that your entire focus is on getting to the CEO's seat, and don't give the impression that your long-term goal is completely different from this job. Both imply that you may not give your best work because your focus won't be here.

Keep your answer **general**: "It's difficult to predict exactly where I'll want to be long-term, but I know I want to continue to learn and develop my skills and achieve in this field. I am good at what I do, and that is rewarding. I know that as I grow more, I'll want to move into roles of greater responsibility, whether that's added responsibility in this position or in a higher-level position down the line."

What changes have you made in working with others to be more effective at work?

This question looks at your willingness to **recognize areas where you need to improve** and execute those necessary changes in a successful way. Don't choose things you were weak on that are

central to your success in this job. There's no reason to insert doubts about your ability to do the job into this conversation. Choose **small things that you improved on because you wanted to** (not because your boss told you to) that had a positive, lasting impact for you.

Here are a few examples:

- I improved my **communication skills** by becoming a better listener, and I have developed excellent working relationships with my colleagues.

- I learned about a **technical area** I had no experience in so that I could **communicate better** with our support department. They seem to appreciate it.

- When I first started out, I used to get upset by others' disagreements and arguments in the office. I learned to step back and distance myself in order to **keep calm** and not let it affect my work or my **positive outlook**. It's kept me on good terms with everyone in the office, too!

- At one time, I was constantly interrupted and pulled every which way by a variety of people coming to me with various requests. So I learned to **set priorities**, and instead of immediately moving to address whatever problem they came to me with, I looked at how that fit into my priority list for the day and planned accordingly. As a result, I am much less stressed and much **more productive**.

- It wasn't necessarily a problem for me, but I am **always looking for ways to improve** and so I realized that I could become a better **time manager**. I looked at my day, figured out where I tended to be most productive at which tasks, and set up a routine. This helped me plan more effectively for meetings with colleagues, and give more accurate dates for completion of projects. It's worked well. I'm very **organized, productive, and easy for others to work with**.

What circumstances bring you here today?

This is a great opening interview question, maybe better than "Tell me about yourself." This question gives them a lot of insight into what will make you happy and what has made you unhappy and **why you are looking for a job**. The important thing to remember here is to **never go negative** in your answer.

They want to hear that you are **running TO something**, like more responsibility, a chance to use increased skill sets, or just something different than you were doing).

They do not want to hear that you are running FROM something, like a boss you can't get along with or a company that doesn't appreciate you or whatever.

So you must explain this in terms of: "The reason why am here is, in my current role I'm doing fantastic. I'm enjoying the work there but I don't get to use the skill sets that I developed at ABC. I don't get to use the experiences that I had at XYZ. I want an opportunity to do LMNOP."

Or, "I'm here because my former company went through a series of layoffs and cut 30% of the workforce and I got caught in the cuts. I think it turned out to be a stroke of luck for me, though, because although I was enjoyed my work there, I didn't get to use my skill sets in XYZ, and this job would really benefit from them."

Always **talk about what this job has that attracts you**, and **what you could bring to it as a benefit** to the company—and anything you can mention using **numbers, dollars and percentages** of what you been able to do and how you'd like to do more of that, will help.

What do you do to grow your skills and knowledge of the job/industry?

Employers want to hire people who continuously learn, grow and improve. It means that you are probably a self-starter, and a good communicator. It means that you are invested in your career and striving for success. It also increases your value, because the more you know,  the more you can do to make money for the company.

There are any number of ways you could talk about that you use to grow your skills and knowledge:

- Read books, journals or industry newsletters
- Take classes / get certifications
- Attend workshops, conferences or seminars
- Watch online videos
- Participate in LinkedIn group discussions
- Volunteer doing something that relates to your job

Whatever you choose to mention, be prepared to **give an example** of something you learned there that helped you be more successful in your job or how it will help you be successful in this one.

What do you expect from this job?

What they really want to know is, why do you want to work *here*? What's in it for you? What aspects of this job appeal to you and why?

You must have done your research in order to answer this question, because you need to be able to explain why THIS job, with this company, is the one for you.

With every answer you give, you should give them another reason to want to hire you, so part of what you say you want or expect from this job should always be **a chance to benefit this company**:

"I expect that in this job, I'll utilize my XYZ skill set to help you accomplish A, B, and C."

Or you could say:

"I expect that because I can utilize my ABC skill set in this role, and be successful and help move you forward, that I will be extremely happy and productive here."

Along with pointing out your **skills match**, point out **what it is that you like** about this particular company:

"I expect to be excited to get up and come to work every day because I will be working at a job that is a great fit for me because of X, Y, and Z, at a great company I've read so many good things about."

Maybe this company:

- Does work you're especially excited about
- Provides a product or service you love
- Fosters a sense of community you can't wait to be a part of

Whatever it is, say it with sincerity.

Here is your chance to **express your genuine enthusiasm** for the job and sum up why you're a great fit for it.

What gets you up in the morning?

For many people, what really gets them up in the morning and motivates them to get on with the day is a personal thing—maybe it's your kids, or your love of life, or your goal of early retirement. In a social setting, these are acceptable and even noble answers. In an interview setting, they are not your best choices. (The worst answer of all is money.)

In an interview, you always want to **keep the focus on your fit for the job**, even with personal questions like these. Good things to mention are **why you like your work**, why this job in particular is a **good match** for you and why you would **enjoy** it. Show your enthusiasm for the job here—it makes you more likeable.

So a good answer might sound like:

"I am one of the lucky few people in the world who gets to get up and do work I love to do. I know that I am good at my job, and I love the feeling of overcoming challenges and being successful. That gives me a sense of accomplishment that makes me excited to get up in the morning and happy when I go to bed at night."

You might mention that you are motivated by:

- **Meeting goals** (like when you met the goal for X last year and were recognized for it)
- **Being recognized** for doing a great job (like when you won 'Most Valuable Employee')
- **Making difficult sales** (like when you landed the customer that everyone said you couldn't)
- **A positive and supportive work environment** (like the one that this company is known for)
- **Competition** (which is why you enjoyed being named #1 out of 135 sales reps in your company)
- **The chance to come up with creative solutions to complex problems** (like you did when you got to be on the team tasked with X in your company and you created Y solution)
- **Knowing that the work you do makes a positive difference in someone's life** (like when you help someone be healthier, save money, reach a goal, etc.)

Talk about something that truly motivates you that is a major factor in this job so you can demonstrate that you are a good fit for it. Back up what you say with an example or an accomplishment that adds credibility and sincerity to your statement.

What have you learned from all the different roles you've had?

This question is just as open-ended as "Tell me about yourself" and just as easy to make a mistake with. When they ask you this, they do not want you to talk about a greater truth you learned or a lesson that changed your life, and they really don't want a long random list of everything you picked up here and there.

Now is the time for you to talk about **when and how you acquired the skill sets and experience that make you a perfect fit for *this* job**.

How have you developed professionally into someone they would be interested in hiring now for this job?

It's important that you **be strategic** and think about **the best answer to this question for YOU**.

Think about what in your **background, experience, or skill sets** is most interesting to this employer:

- What are the key **requirements** or **competencies** of this job?
- What are the **problems** they need to have **addressed** and **solved**?
- What are their **goals**?

Use your knowledge of what this employer is interested in to choose things in your own background to highlight.

For instance, when interviewing for a **sales job**, you might say,

"In my first job, my manager gave me the book SPIN Selling by Neil Rackham and reading it changed my life. I went from mediocre sales numbers to ranking among the highest in the company as a practically brand-new hire.

SPIN Selling
by Neil Rackham

·NEIL RACKHAM·

SPIN SELLING

SITUATION · PROBLEM · IMPLICATION · NEED-PAYOFF

THE BEST-VALIDATED SALES METHOD AVAILABLE TODAY. DEVELOPED FROM RESEARCH STUDIES OF 35,000 SALES CALLS. USED BY THE TOP SALES FORCES ACROSS THE WORLD.

amazon.com

In my next job, I went into selling a much more technical product, which meant I had to fill in gaps in my background to be able to know my product and discuss it intelligently with my customers.

But what I learned from that is that I can train myself—I don't need my employer to do it for me, and learning those new things boosted my confidence level, too.

In my current job, I worked with someone who happened to be a tremendous time manager and watching her, I learned a lot about how to prioritize tasks and organize my day so that my productivity has gone up I would estimate about 30%."

So what you've told this interviewer in your answer is that:

(1) You are a great sales rep who achieved a **significant ranking** early on;

(2) you can **train yourself** on the product even if it is an unfamiliar one; and

(3) you are **organized and efficient with your time.**

Maybe what you need to point out is that you:

- **Learned a new software** that this company uses
- **Developed customer service techniques** that help you retain customers at a 20% higher level than before (and this job description puts a high value on customer retention)
- **Created market trials** that helped you hone your skill at matching products to customer need
- **Learned a particular procedure** that helped you increase X

Whatever it is, make sure that **what you learned is something that this employer could use as a reason to hire you.**

What historical figure do you admire and why?

There are a lot of historical figures that I admire. In an interview, I would choose one that helps me demonstrate a **desirable work quality or fit for the job**.

A historical figure I admire is Joseph Juran, the Italian economist who developed the Pareto Principle, known as the 80/20 Rule. I use the 80/20 Rule daily to **prioritize tasks for maximum results**. It helps me accomplish more in a shorter amount of time and achieve greater success.

For instance, when I was in sales, I used the 80/20 Rule to identify which customers generated the most revenue, and which actions generated the most sales. Then I made sure that I spent most of my time on the things that produced the most results.

So not only have I chosen an admirable historical figure, I have **tied my choice to a positive trait in my work** and another selling point for me. You could also choose:

- **a leader in your field**
- someone who's personal life is an example of an **admirable character trait**
- someone who exemplifies great **leadership**

Try to keep your choice as **uncontroversial** as possible— **no religious or political figures**. Even if you truly admire whoever it is, it's better in this situation to **play it safe**.

80/20 Rule

A long, LONG time ago, an Italian economist named Pareto noticed that 80% of the wealth in Italy was held by 20% of the people. Joseph Juran took Pareto's Principle and successfully applied it to quality management--and the 80/20 Rule was born.

The 80/20 Rule says (among other things) that 80% of sales come from 20% of customers, or that **80% of your results come from 20% of your effort.**

It's about productivity and identifying the significant tasks/actions that contribute most to it. Prioritize the most important tasks, and you become super-efficient and effective. You will spend time on the things that matter.

What if you worked for someone who managed to take credit for all your great ideas? How would you handle it?

Hopefully, by asking this question, the interviewer is only trying to get a sense of **how you deal with conflict** and not warning you that they are about to take credit for all your great ideas.

With conflict questions in general, the interviewer wants to know several things:

- How do you see **your role** at work?
- What is your **communication style**?

- Do you remain **calm**?
- Do you **confront issues** head on?
- Do you try to **keep the peace** at all costs?
- Do you take things to HR, or handle them yourself?
- How do you **approach the situation** and how do you **come up with solutions**?

I probably would try to inject a little humor into this answer:

"Well, part of my job is certainly to make my boss look good, and my great ideas are part of that. I certainly want my boss to be recognized and rewarded for having the good sense to hire me!"

Or, you could just cut to the bottom line:

"Well, part of my job is to provide great ideas that make my boss look good. If I were being rewarded by my boss with raises and promotions, I would be happy."

(And then I would probably go home and get on LinkedIn or Facebook and try to find people who have worked for this person before and see if they would ever work for them again!)

What is one thing you'd like to do better? What is your plan for accomplishing that?

This question is virtually the same as, "What is your greatest weakness?" With all weakness questions, be sincere (no obviously 'fake,' clichéd answers) but focus your answer on something that is:

(1) a **minor part** of your job you are **already improving** on
(2) a **personal weakness** but a **professional strength**
(3) something that would be a **benefit to you later in your career** but that you don't necessarily need now

(**All 'strength' questions should be directly tied to key parts of your job.**)

You can't say that there's nothing you'd like to do better—that reveals you as someone who thinks they're already perfect and has no room to grow.

You can't say that you have a major flaw that would directly affect your job—like that you are uncomfortable meeting new people even though you're in sales, or that you struggle with time management and prioritization if you are a project manager, or that you need to pay more attention to details if you are an accountant.

So what should you say? Maybe something like:

"I always want to improve my **communication skills**, because that's the bottom-line key skill everything else depends on. It doesn't matter how good you are technically if you can't communicate effectively with the people you work with and for. So, I regularly read books and articles about improving communication skills, and I put what I learn into practice every day."

****

"I would like to **handle stress better**. I've been making great progress with that personally by making sure I eat right and work out every day and professionally by reading books on time management and prioritization that have taught me a lot about planning and strategizing so that I am always in control of the situation, which is a tremendous stress-reliever."

****

"I'd like to be a **better public speaker**, because that's a skill everyone should have, and it would make me stronger running meetings and giving presentations at work. I frequently watch YouTube videos as tutorials and I watch great public speakers as examples of what to do. I also joined Toastmasters so I can practice."

What is the last book you read for fun? (Or, what is your favorite book?)

Interviewers frequently want to know:

(1) **If** you read, because someone who reads is generally seen as **intelligent, curious, and interested in personal growth**

(2) **What kinds of things** you spend your time reading, because that says a lot about you, your character, and your priorities

This particular question is a personal one, because it's asking what you read for fun. The interviewer is looking at your personality and whether you would be a **good cultural fit** within the organization.

It's OK to answer this question with titles you really enjoy—within reason. Don't talk about any book that might raise an eyebrow. **Keep it mainstream and socially acceptable**.

Maybe the book you mention is:

- **the fiction one the latest blockbuster movie is based on**, so you show that you are socially current
- **a non-fiction one on the best-seller lists** that everyone is talking about
- **a book that is important for your field** and you read it for fun because you really like your work

Briefly mention the title and why you enjoy the book—maybe it's got a lot of **humor** (because you have a sense of humor) or it's filled **with plot-twisting suspense** (because it keeps your very intelligent mind engaged) or it's introduced some **new ideas** to you (because you like learning new ways to think about things).

Be prepared to talk about the book you mention. I once interviewed someone who mentioned a book I had just read, so I asked him about something in it. It became crystal clear right then that he did not know what I was talking about and had **lied to me** about reading the book. Right then, I was **DONE** with that candidate.

I always like to use humor in job interviews if I can, but it's probably not a good idea to say, "The last book I read is a book on how to answer interview questions!" It's funny, but it isn't helpful. The books I have recommended to you throughout this book, however, are great things for you to pick up and read quickly before your interview!

What is the most courageous action or unpopular stand that you have ever taken?

This question could apply to you whether you are a manager or an individual contributor. Managers often have to make tough decisions, and as an individual contributor you might face a situation where someone asks you to cut corners or otherwise slide around the rules rather than stick to them.

This really is a question to measure your **integrity, courage, and leadership**, and you need to show that you are not afraid to make difficult decisions when they are in the best interests of your job or the well-being of the company.

Use the **STAR format** to tell this story:

Situation or Task –

Set the scene. What was going on? What was the **conflict**? Why were you faced with this problem? What **factors** affected the situation? What **risks** did you face?

This situation could be anything...maybe you needed to lay off a certain percentage of your workforce, maybe you needed to set a new policy you knew would make some employees unhappy, or maybe you were leading a team where one member wasn't pulling their weight. Maybe your boss asked you to do something you weren't comfortable with. Maybe this was your decision to leave the company and start your own business.

Action –

What did you do to address the situation? How did you think about it? Did you ask for help or input from co-workers, counterparts, your boss, or mentors? How did you come to the decision you did and what did you do to execute on that decision?

Maybe you had a private conversation with the person causing the problem, maybe you weighed the pros and cons, maybe you gathered data to evaluate to inform your decision, or maybe you more clearly explained the positives that would come from this decision. Walk them through the process.

Result –

What happened as a result of your decision? Was it the right decision? Did the situation get better?

Ideally, this is where you explain the **triumphant happy ending** to your story where everybody came around to your way of thinking, and maybe you even were recognized for your action. Or, maybe this is where you got fired, and this is your chance to tell the story.

What is the most important thing you're looking for in a company/job besides salary?

The very best answer to this question of what you're looking for is a list of things that this position offers. You'd say it like this:

"What I'm looking for is actually a very good match for this position...that's why I was so excited about interviewing with you."

Then, you can **move into specifics** about why this job and this company is such a good match. You need the **job description** for this, but it will also help you if you have done your **research on the company** before the interview.

For example:

"What this job (or company) offers that others don't is A, B, and C. I believe it's a unique opportunity to utilize my skills in X, Y, and Z, and that's why I'm particularly excited about it."

Pointing out specific things about this job and this company that genuinely appeal to you will give you the **biggest impact** in your answer.

If you wanted to keep this answer **more generalized**, you could say,

"I want to work for a company where I can enjoy going to work each day, because I can make an impact and be recognized and rewarded for it."

What is your biggest weakness that's really a weakness and not a secret strength?

The first thing you learn in Answering Interview Questions 101 is "don't tell them anything negative about yourself." And now here is this hiring manager asking you to go against everything you've learned about selling yourself for the job and tell him something truly negative about you. Why? Because hiring you is a risk for this person, and trying to find the dirt about you before you're hired is risk-assessment and evaluation. Are you worth the risk?

This question also tells you that this interviewer has heard "I'm a perfectionist" and "I work too hard" a few too many times. So they're looking for a real weakness, and you have to say something because everyone has at least one—what can you say?

Whatever you do, **don't give a weakness that would have a direct negative impact on your job performance.**

For instance, no project manager should say their weakness is organization or delegation, no accountant should say that their weakness is attention to detail, and no customer service rep should say that they have anger issues.

One of the **best strategies** for this question is to give **a real weakness that causes you problems in other areas of your life but doesn't affect your performance on the job**.

For instance, I always gave 'impatience' as my weakness. I am impatient, and it has caused me significant problems in my personal life with my family and friends. However, that same impatience made me super successful in my role as a sales rep because I could not stand waiting around for the sale. I pushed for it every time (and I usually got it).

You could give a weakness that you **actually have**, but that you have a solid, working way to **overcome**: "I get so involved in my work that I lose track of what time it is. I'm so thankful for cell phone alarms or I'd never make a meeting on time!"

'Fear of public speaking' is a real weakness that is also a very **common** one that the hiring manager can probably relate to. Unless your job involves giving presentations on a daily or weekly basis, you can safely get by with this one.

What is your favorite website?

Do not say:

- Amazon (although, who doesn't love Amazon??)--because they'll think you online shop all day
- ESPN -- same thing—are you working or checking scores on last night's game?
- Facebook (statistics say people spend 3 hours a day on Facebook—this is a real worry for supervisors)
- Any website that trumpets your political views
- Pinterest (you could get lost in that maze forever...)

Unless you are in a field that relies heavily on social media or other internet-based activity, this question is a general one similar to 'What's your favorite book?' It's just trying to uncover a bit more about you, your personality, and your preferences.

Choose a **useful, practical website** that contributes to your professional success. This would be the website you wouldn't rush to close if your boss walked up to your computer. You could choose:

- a **specialty website** that concentrates in **your career** arena (like AdAge for media and advertising news and trends, or Inc. for sales and marketing tips and tricks)
- a **trend-watcher website** that helps you forecast and make marketing decisions
- **Lifehacker.com** for tips and shortcuts to get things done smarter and more efficiently
- any **mainstream news** site
- **Forbes.com** for business and professional development
- **YouTube** or **Ted.com** for instructional videos

I would answer this question very briefly—naming the website with a quick mention of what it is, if it isn't an extremely common one.

A nice way to end this answer is to say something like, "Do you know of a new one I should know about?" or "What's yours?" that **tosses the conversational ball back to them**. Maybe you'll learn about a great new website!

What qualities in your co-workers bother you most? What do you appreciate most?

On the surface, this sounds like it's a personality question or a cultural fit question. In reality, it's a **measure of your attitude** and **your ability to get along with others**. For this reason, you want to answer both of these questions very **positively**.

However, I do not think that you have to do the obviously fake, "I can't think of anything that bothers me about my co-workers." I believe that answer is the same kind of bad answer as "My greatest weakness is that I just work too darn hard." It just sounds false.

Everyone can think of things that others do that bother them. The trick is balance. Never tell a story about how one person irritated you—make it about a **general quality**. Tell them something that bothers you, but limit it to one thing and make that one thing **something that would bother anyone**.

For instance, I would say, "I don't particularly appreciate **negative attitudes** because they're not helpful to anyone— the person who's complaining or the person listening to it. I believe that instead of complaining about a problem, you should focus on how to fix it."

Then move right into the **positive**: "I've been very lucky to have worked with some great people in my career who have demonstrated qualities I appreciate a lot, like working hard, being knowledgeable, and having a positive attitude."

Keep both answers general and add a few more attributes on the things you appreciate than the things you don't.

The words you say and the things you focus on say more about you than about whatever you're talking about—so make sure that you present yourself in a positive, professional way.

What tools or techniques do you use to stay organized and increase your productivity?

Organization is key to true productivity...just ask anyone who can't find something they need to time how long it takes them to look for it, or anyone who missed a deadline because they forgot about it.

Anyone can say they are organized and productive, but not everyone is. This question asks for **evidence**. It's a simple question with a simple answer.

If you have a **great system for staying organized**, tell them about it.

- Are you a Franklin Planner kind of person, a traditional "To Do" list maker or an app user?
- Do you use Google Apps, Outlook, or Remember the Milk?
- Do you use a CRM (Customer Relationship Management) system such as Zoho, Help Desk, or Salesforce.com?
- Do you use a project management system such as Team Support or Basecamp?
- Do you mainly use your computer or your smart phone?

Using an **online scheduling software** or some other **online gadget** to stay organized can make you seem up-to-date and computer savvy, but **what really counts is that it works** (and that you show that it works). What keeps you organized? How do you **manage your workload**?

You might also quickly mention how you **prioritize tasks**, how you make sure you **meet deadlines**, and how you don't let anything slip through the cracks with a **reminder system**.

A nice addition to the end of your answer here is an example of **how many** projects/things/people you are able to keep track of with your system. Keep it short but descriptive. Remember, **quantification is powerful**.

What will your job references say about you?

You absolutely need to **know what your references will say about you** before you give their names to a potential employer.

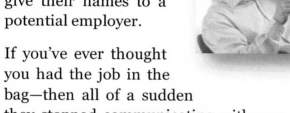

If you've ever thought you had the job in the bag—then all of a sudden they stopped communicating with you, it may be that your references brought you down.

How to make sure your references help you get the job:

- **choose good quality references** (people you have worked for or reported to are the best ones)
- **ask if they're comfortable giving you a reference**, what they might say about you, if they'll be available, and the best way to contact them
- **prep them** before they are called by telling them what to focus on ("Hey, I'm interviewing for X job doing ABC...can you mention the work I did on X, and that I'm amazing?")

But this employer won't expect that you can read the minds of your references, so what they are really asking for is a **list of your strengths**.

This is easy to match up with what your references will talk about if you coach them before they're called.

If you know that one will mention your high-level creativity as demonstrated on a certain project, then you can say, "My references will say that I am extremely creative."

If you know another will be able to speak to your overall skill set, you can say, "My reference will say that this job fits me well because of X, Y, and Z."

If you know another reference would hire you if they could, that is a wonderful thing to report: "My reference would say that they would hire me again in a minute if they could." This is the strongest recommendation of all.

Make sure you're communicating well with your references so you know what they will say about you. The last thing you want is to say something that your references will contradict.

Here's a hint: Go back though your performance appraisals and look for descriptive words. Even better? Pick a few trusted people (mentors, previous bosses, past or current co-workers) and ask them what impression you give to others. What 3 words would they use to describe you? You have to be a little bit brave with this one. It can be difficult to ask. But the answers you get will help you both answer this question and make sure you're projecting the image you want to project in this job search.

What would the person who likes you least in the world say about you?

The person who asks this question really wants to know your **weaknesses**. They might as well say, "What irritating quality are you hiding that's going to show up after you're here for a week?"

As with any weakness question, choose something that is a **real weakness**, most likely in your **personal life**, but provides a **benefit to you in your work life**.

I've always chosen **impatience**, because it's caused me some friction with my family and friends who don't appreciate it, but served me very well as a top sales rep because I couldn't wait to get the sale. Impatience might also be a good quality in someone who needs to drive a team to get something done on deadline.

Another negative quality might be **stubbornness**, which would irritate someone who might have to live with you, but might really be appreciated by a boss who knows you'll stick to the job until it's finished—no matter what.

You might be someone who **isn't particularly good with details**, which drives your spouse crazy, but if you're applying for a job as a manager, you might be needed more for big-picture, strategic thinking and can hire someone to handle details for you. Or you compensate for that by using a killer software program that organizes your life.

Maybe you're **extremely competitive** which has caused you some tense conversations at family gatherings, but makes you an extremely valuable asset in sales and marketing.

Maybe you're a **pessimist**, but that quality of finding flaws and faults has saved your company hundreds of thousands of dollars through avoiding mistakes.

Maybe you've been accused of being **too blunt or direct**, but your direct honesty makes you someone who always tells the truth, even if it is difficult.

You want to be seen as someone who knows you have flaws and doesn't try to act like you don't, but you also want to try and **spin it** so that they can see that **even your flaws can benefit their company**.

What would you do if management made a decision you didn't agree with?

Why would they ask this question? They ask it to see **how you would react in a very difficult situation**. Would you make a fuss? Would you confront your boss? Would you organize a union and overthrow the company?

Here's an answer that shows you are **a *team player* who respects the chain of command**:

"If asked my opinion beforehand, I certainly give it, because it's in my best interests to always apply my best analytical and strategic thinking skills to my company and spot issues before they become problems. If the decision has already been made, there's nothing else to do but live with it. I would assume they made that decision for a reason and I respect that."

What would you do if you found out the company you worked for was doing something illegal?

I might be nervous about a company asking this question, because I'd wonder what can of worms I'd open up by taking this job! Most likely, this is simply a behavioral interview question designed to get at your **values, ethics, and loyalty**.

They don't want you to say you'd become the loudest whistleblower the country's ever seen—what if you were wrong and you damaged the company's reputation?

A calmer, more reasoned response they'd be comfortable with would sound like, "I would report it to my immediate supervisor, or if necessary, the Director or VP, and move up the chain from there. I would want to know if this was an isolated incident involving just a few people, or one person, and not a cultural mindset of the entire organization, and I would follow up with it to see if it gets resolved."

 This shows you're ethical and wouldn't let something illegal and damaging slide, but that you're also loyal and would take a calm approach that assumes it's the fault of only a few and can be corrected.

What would you do if you got behind schedule with your part of a project?

While this is a Behavioral Interview Question that is normally answered using the STAR format, I don't think that I would start telling the interviewer all about a time I got behind schedule. Instead, I would address this problem as a **theoretical possibility** and walk them through a **decision-making process**, taking into account different factors and considering a variety of solutions.

So, for instance, I might say:

"Well, I hate the thought of being the bottleneck in a project, so I try very hard to make sure that never happens.

If it did, the first thing I would do is determine **why** I was behind, because you can't identify a good solution without knowing the problem you need to solve.

I would look to see if I got behind because the work was more complicated than anticipated or because

I got sidetracked by a more urgent matter, or whatever the issue was.

Next, I would consider how far along I was in the project and how far behind I was. I would **consider a variety of options**, including working **overtime** to get caught up, **delegating** some of my tasks so the work could get done faster, looking for ways to be more **efficient** with my process, or maybe even **reprioritizing** what had to be done by the deadline and what could be added later.

When you're behind, the most critical thing to do is **communicate and control expectations**, so I would notify my boss of the problem, the solution I had come up with for it, and any new projected end dates to see if she approved or if she had any additional solutions.

Assuming all was a go, then I would execute and work as hard as I could to bring my part of the project to a successful conclusion as fast as possible."

Answering the question this way gives the interviewer a lot of information about how you **manage your time**, **prioritize tasks**, and **critically think through options**.

What would you do if you made an important business decision and a co-worker challenged it?

This question gets to **how you deal with criticism**.

Give the interviewer the idea that you're confident enough to be open to criticism or challenges without getting stopped in your tracks with anger or indecision.

In this case, I would say, "I would take this person aside and ask why they felt the way they did, because I'm always interested in hearing the pros and cons of a decision so that I can make the best one. I never like the idea of making a mistake, but if I do, I want to correct it. If what they told me made no difference to my decision or it was something I'd already considered, I'd thank them for their input, let it go, and move on."

You want to show that you are **thoughtful, coachable, and professional** even in the face of criticism of your decisions, as well as confident enough to stick by a good one.

What would you look to accomplish in the first 30 days/60 days/90 days on the job?

Congratulations, this is your lead-in for your **30-60-90-Day Plan**! Having a plan written out for the interview, that you can look at with the hiring manager and discuss, is **THE best interview tool you could ever use**. It shows that you are someone with **drive, ambition, initiative, enthusiasm, good strategic thinking skills, good prioritization skills, and good problem-solving skills** who can **set goals** and know what steps will **achieve** them.

With this question, they're looking to visualize you in this role, and your plan will help them do that.

You say, "I'm so glad you asked that. I've actually created an outline of what I think my action steps and goals should be for the first 30, 60, and 90 days of this job and I'd like to go over it with you and get your feedback."

You'll start with what you need to do in the **first 30 days** to familiarize yourself with the company:

- Training
- Meeting co-workers, team or other departments
- Learning systems, procedures, or software
- Getting your feet wet with your first projects or customers

After you discuss this for a few minutes, you'll move on to the next 30 days (the **60-day** section):

- Get up to speed with your job
- Get feedback on your progress
- Start going off more on your own

Then, you'll begin discussing the last 30 days (the **90-day** part):

- Start bigger projects
- Set longer-term goals
- Establish new procedures
- Make improvements

As much as you can, add details that are specific to this company (such as the name of the person you'd report to or the name of their training program). Think about what would make you successful from Day 1 in this job.

Key to a Great Interview!
A 30-60-90-day plan helps make it an easy decision to hire you!
Find out more about 30-60-90-Day Plans at http://CareerConfidential.com

What would your direct reports say about you?

This question explores your **leadership qualities**. What is your leadership style? What do you do that makes you a good leader?

Great things to mention that they might say are that you **set clear expectations**, you are **fair**, you're a good **communicator** and a willing **teacher**, you give balanced **feedback**, and that you are extremely **knowledgeable** about your industry.

Choose **2 or 3 things that accurately describe you** and say, "My direct reports would say that I am X and Y."

If you happen to have any **evidence** that supports this, offer it. Possibly this could be a direct report who is serving as a **reference**, or a **performance review** discussing your leadership qualities, or an **assessment of your group or team's performance** compared to others in the company (the idea being that if your team was especially successful as a whole, you must be doing something right).

What, as an organization, can we offer that is better than your current employer?

Your interviewer wants to know that you are genuinely interested in and enthusiastic about working for their company. They don't really want you to compare and contrast the two companies—and besides, if you get into doing that you can veer off track very quickly into badmouthing your current company which is always a no-no.

They want to know **what attracts you to this job**, based on your research and your own opinion—so answer that question.

Your answer should be, "I am especially interested in this job at this company because..." and then give **at least 3 very sincere, positive reasons why you are excited about this job**.

One reason should address the fact that **this job is a good fit for you professionally and culturally**. You are interested in that, after all. So, talk about how your skills will make you successful there:

"...this organization is a perfect fit for me. You need X, Y, and Z, and I have all of those plus ABC. That's going to make me very effective working here, and I am excited about the opportunity. I've been reading about the company and it seems like a great fit for my personality, values, and work style."

Then move into a reason that addresses a **particular professional aspect** they offer that others don't. This is where your **research** is going to come in particularly handy, because the more specific you can be, the better. This could be any number of things:

- They work with a **particular customer**, slice of the **market**, **procedure**, or **software**.
- They are expanding into a **new market**.
- They are **leaders** in their field.
- They are just **starting up** so they have all kinds of room to grow quickly.
- They have a great **reputation.**
- They create **cutting-edge products**.
- They are known for having the **highest-quality** X, and you want to be a part of that.

End your answer with a more personal reason that this job appeals to you, which could also be any number of things:

- They emphasize **employee development** and you are always interested in learning new things and growing professionally.
- They are known for being a great place to work in terms of **community**, and you think of work as an extended family.
- You **personally use their products** and are jazzed about the idea of contributing to their creation, distribution or sale.
- You'll have considerably **more autonomy and responsibility** with this job which will make your work life more rewarding.
- It's **closer to your house**, which will make your commute very short and add to your quality of life.
- It requires **less travel**, because you are ready to be in your own bed more often.

Do you research, be specific, be positive, and show your sincere enthusiasm for working in this role, for this organization.

What's your favorite dish, and how would you convince someone who hated an ingredient in it to try it?

I think the 'favorite dish' part of this question is a throwaway part. They don't really care what your favorite dish is (mine is pizza). What they care about is **your ability to construct a compelling argument in the face of strong resistance**. This could be a good question for sales jobs, management jobs where they're trying to change the culture, or any other jobs where persuasion would be required.

To convince someone of something, it often works to use the 'feel-felt-found' argument. (I know how you feel...I felt the same way...this is what I found.)

In my case, I would use sweet potatoes:

"I didn't like sweet potatoes either, until I was 30 years old. I thought they were gross and disgusting, like you do—but the ones that you tried aren't like what I want you to try. Those were in a can and disgusting and you are right. But these are fresh sweet potatoes that have been baked with honey and butter and brown sugar all over them and they are incredible.

Sometimes when you find an ingredient that you don't like, in another situation you may very well like it. And sweet potatoes are so incredibly good for you and have so much Vitamin A that they are worth another shot. You need to always try different things and have different foods to eat."

So I've **established common ground**, I've **engaged their emotions and senses**, I've used **logic** as well as a **good nutrition** argument.

When would you be available to start?

This question requires a straightforward, factual response.

If you can start as soon as they're ready for you to start, then say that.

If you need to give notice to your employer, then let them know how much notice you are required to give—usually this is two weeks.

However, **don't box yourself into a corner** by giving them a firm date, because you don't know exactly when you'll have a firm offer in your hand, and you don't want to cut yourself too short and burn bridges at your current company.

So say, "I would be able to give two weeks' notice as soon as I have a firm offer, so it would be two weeks after that."

If it's longer than two weeks, you need to have a very good reason for that. It could be that your **contract** requires a longer time frame, so say so. If you are in the **middle of a big project** and think it's only fair to finish it first, you could give that reason—but you run a risk. Either they'll think you are exceptionally **loyal** and dedicated, or they'll think you're **not serious** about wanting to work for them. They will definitely think you're not serious about wanting to work there if you give them an extended time frame. It may make them think you are **shopping around**, and will only take their offer if you don't get something better.

If there is a question of when you could start, or you think they might be in a particular **hurry** to hire someone, answer the question with a question: "When do you need someone to start?" Their answer might change your answer, depending on how badly you want this job.

Who are our competitors?

An interviewer who asks this wants to see:

- if you have done your homework and **researched their company** before the interview
- if you are really **as familiar with this arena/product/service** as you should be
- what else you mention on this topic that tells them more about **what you can offer them in terms of organizational advantage**

This is a big question in any **sales job**, but it can easily come up in other fields. Not only should you know the **competitors' names**, you should know **a few of the most important facts** about them in relation to this company and the market.

You can get this information through **Google** and **LinkedIn**, and by talking to your personal network or LinkedIn groups. The more **specific** you can be, the better.

If you've worked for their competitors, be careful about disclosing anything that would violate a confidentiality or non-compete agreement.

What would be useful to mention **along with the names**?

- **Differences** and **similarities**
- **Recent sales comparisons**
- **Market share/ tactics**
- A specific **struggle in a certain market** or with a certain product
- **Reviews, news stories**
- This company's place in **popular rankings or lists**
- This company's efforts to **gain an advantage over their competitors**
- Why this company is (in your opinion) **better than the others**

If you can, **offer a general suggestion** for an activity or strategy that would help against their competition, such as:

- **Marketing opportunities**
- **Threats**
- **Current trends**

The biggest point of all this is to show that you have done your research on the company and the industry and that you can have an informed, intelligent discussion about it.

Key to a Great Interview

SWOT Analysis

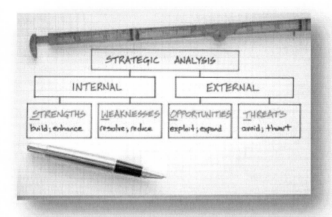

SWOT is a strategic planning tool that stands for:

- **Strengths** (attributes helpful to achieving the objective)
- **Weaknesses** (attributes harmful to achieving the objective)
- **Opportunities** (external conditions that will be helpful to achieving the objective)
- **Threats** (external obstacles or conditions that will harm the process)

Doing a SWOT analysis on the company demonstrates your drive, commitment, and skills, along with helping you create a better 30/60/90-day plan.

Who are the influencers in your life?

The people who influence you in your life obviously have a direct impact on your **character**, your **values**, and your **behavior**.

Who you choose to mention as an influencer tells the interviewer a lot about you personally—what you value, and what you aspire to.

What you need to do here is **give an example of one or two influencers** and say **why** they are an influence in your life.

For instance, I would say, "My influencers would be my parents, who taught me how to work hard, to challenge myself, and to make smart decisions, and my mentors, who I have chosen myself to be my teachers and coaches in different areas of my professional life. I value those relationships and make the time to maintain them so that I can always be learning and growing, and I try to return the favor and help them out as much as I can with information and insights of my own."

Now, I've had many, many people that I've learned from in my life and career—too many to list. The ones I choose tell an employer that I'm **smart**, **ambitious**, I **work hard**, and I am always **striving to improve myself**.

You may have had many influencers or those that you admire, too. What have you learned from them? What parts of that make you better at your job? This could be so many things:

- Dedication
- Drive
- Ethics
- Loyalty
- Integrity
- Hard work
- Service

- Leadership
- Positive Attitude
- Confidence
- Communication Skills
- Courage

What do you want this employer to know and remember about you and your character?

Whatever you want this employer to know about you as a person, that's what you should highlight in your answer by choosing which influencers to mention and what specifically you learned from them.

Who do you follow on Twitter and why?

 First, are you on Twitter? Do you Tweet? This question uncovers how much you participate in **social media** in general, how **computer- and internet-savvy** you are, and who you think is important enough to spend your valuable time on, finding out what they think.

Who you follow on Twitter says a lot about you and what is a **priority** in your life. Are you only following celebrities (I hope not) or looking for relevant and helpful information? Do you follow those who contribute to your personal or professional development? Are you following the **major players** and **influencers in your field**?

Here is a drop in the bucket of interesting people/organizations to follow on Twitter:

- **Brian Tracy** – world-renowned speaker and coach for positive change in business and life
- **TED Talks** – mini lessons by experts in a variety of fields
- **Brian Solis** – digital analyst, sociologist and futurist focuses on business-consumer relationship and social media strategy

- **Steve Randy Waldman** – Private investor with insights on economics and finance
- **Mark Hunter** – The Sales Hunter who tweets motivational insights on sales, leadership, and more
- **DARPA** (Defense Advanced Research Projects Agency) – develops new technology for the military
- **Neil deGrasse Tyson** – astrophysicist who tweets about science and makes great jokes

You can browse interests through a variety of topics to see any names you might recognize.

If you aren't on Twitter, it's worth it to get an account now and start exploring. You really can pick up a lot of useful news and information.

If you aren't on Twitter and aren't going to be, it's OK to say that but then mention other social media you may participate in and how that is beneficial for you.

Why did you get into this line of work? (choose this as a career)

This is not just a friendly, ice-breaking kind of question (any more than any other interview question is). It's true that they are asking about your motivations, interests and values:

- **Why** do you do what you do?
- What **influenced** your decision?
- Do you have any particular **talents** that made this an easy choice?
- Is this related to a life-long **interest** or **hobby** for you?

Think this question through just a little bit further, with the knowledge that the job search and interview is a sales process, the hiring manager is the 'customer' and you are the 'product,' and you'll realize that what they really want to know is:

- **Are you interested in and enthusiastic about what you do?** If so, you will be a better employee who is more successful and produces more success for the company.

- **Why and how does this apply to your fit for the job?** You need to connect the dots for them...if you have a particular ability or talent that encouraged you to pursue this career, give an example of how you have been successful using that talent.

For instance, here's my answer:

"When I first started out, I entered the field of medical sales. I loved the medical field but didn't want to be a doctor. I enjoy meeting new people and I loved the challenge of persuading someone to buy my product.

When I began recruiting for the medical field, I was looking to reduce my travel because I had a young son. I had been a high-level sales manager in the medical arena and knew how difficult it could be to identify and evaluate good candidates to hire. I knew that I could do that very well because of my particular experience. This way, I kept my hand in the field, I still got to speak with people all over the world, I still got to persuade and influence, but this time it was my clients and candidates.

I started my own company and became a career coach, because I knew that I had a passion for helping others and wanted to expand it outside of just the medical sales arena. I show job seekers how to get hired. Now I get to persuade and influence on a global scale through helping tens of thousands of job seekers in over 90 countries. I get a lot of satisfaction out of knowing I've helped them get hired and receiving their phone calls and emails that thank me for my help."

****

Try to show that **you chose this career on purpose** instead of a random accident—but if you did just happen to stumble into this line of work at least talk about what a **happy accident** it was and how you've made **deliberate steps to grow and learn** more since then.

Why don't you want to give me your salary requirements?

Salary is one of the most difficult and delicate topics of the entire job search and interview process. I always recommend to my candidates that they try to **completely avoid any discussion of salary** until after the company has decided they want to hire you. Why? Because you want them to fall in love with you and have to have you before you tell them how much it's going to cost. This puts you in a much better bargaining position when it's time to talk dollars.

Whether you are interviewing with HR or a hiring manager, they are going to ask about your salary requirements, both to see if they can afford you and to see how little they can get you for. Your job is to **deflect** as much as possible.

By the time they get to this question, you have deflected many times and they are pushing for an answer. You have several good options:

(1) Say, "I'm **uncomfortable giving you a salary requirement until I know all the factors.** I'm not sure if we've covered all the responsibilities and goals for this position yet, or what the other elements in your compensation package are. Can you tell me what the entire package would be?" Whatever you might have earned in another position isn't really relevant to what is fair for this job. Even similar jobs will have different responsibilities and goals in different companies. Other factors in a compensation package (healthcare, profit sharing, bonuses, perks, etc.) can make up for a less-than-desired salary.

Key to a Great Interview

Negotiating the Best Salary

Find out everything you need to know about navigating salary questions and negotiating the best compensation and benefits here:

Negotiating Your Salary:
How to Make $1000 a Minute

by Jack Chapman

amazon.com

(2) Go ahead and tell them something. Do your **research on salary ranges** for this role, in this size company, in this industry, in this area of the country. Good

research sites include Salary.com, Glassdoor.com and Payscale.com.

Tell them that you found out that the range for this job is between X and Y. "Y" should be the top of the range and "X" should be in the middle. This way, you are **setting a bias** that is skewed toward a higher end number. It's an 'anchor' that pulls the entire direction of the negotiation towards it.

(3) Say, "My **salary requirements aren't relevant** unless we have decided that I am a good fit for this role. If you have decided that you'd like to hire me, I'd love to talk compensation and benefits with you. If you need to know more about my skills and qualifications first, then let's talk more about that. What else would you like to know?"

(4) **Keep refusing** and say, "I know that you must have a range budgeted for this position. I am sure that **the range you have set will be fair** and commensurate with the responsibilities of this job. **Can you tell me what that range is,** and then I can confirm that I can be comfortable with that range. What is the range?"

Will you be out to take my job?

In larger companies, managers always need to be looking for the one who can take their place so that they can move up. If this is where you are, they might just be checking out your level of ambition. In this situation, I might answer it with humor: "I'm sure by the time that happens, you'll be running the whole company."

In smaller companies, there might be nowhere for this person to go—so if you want an in-house promotion, it will mean kicking them out the door. In this situation, you need to reassure them that you are there to learn and contribute. So say something like:

"Of course not. I'm sure that I'm going to learn a lot from you and that we are going to develop a great working relationship. As long as I keep getting to learn new things and contribute in a meaningful way and being rewarded for that, I'm going to feel great about coming to work here with you every day."

Would you rather be liked or feared?

The best answer is, "Neither. I'd rather be **respected**."

Some interviewers won't accept this and press for a choice.

If I were pressed to choose only one, I would say, "I would rather be liked, because I believe that people go out of their way to help those they like, and feel more invested in our collective success. I think fear is too negative an emotion and wouldn't produce an environment that is creative, innovative, or motivating to do a great job."

However, the interviewer may accept your "respect" answer and follow up with a question about **how you would inspire respect** in your team or employees. One of the best ways to **earn respect** is to ask great questions, to understand the situation before you make decisions. Many managers do more harm than good by jumping to conclusions and make mistakes that hurt individuals and group morale. A manager who makes decisions based on a complete gathering of evidence makes stronger decisions.

You are changing careers. Why should I let you 'experiment' with me and basically pay you to learn on the job?

The very best answer to this question is to say, "That is a good question. I created a 30-60-90-day plan to show you how I can practically flatten my learning curve. It's an outline of what I see as the main action steps and goals that would make me wildly successful in this job."

With this, the hiring manager is probably going to be very curious about what you have come up with, and be willing to look at your plan with you.

When you talk about your first 30 days, you're going to want to emphasize how you will **train yourself** to learn what you need to know. It **won't be a problem for this hiring manager** to worry about, and it **won't slow you down**. If you are changing careers, you will need to do a lot of **research** in order to determine what **books** you should read, what **people** you need to talk to, or even what **courses** you need to take to get up to speed.

When you talk about your next 30 days (the 60-day part), you're going to want to show how your **transferrable skills** will come into play, along with your own self-training to make you a strong performer in this role.

Think about **what your skills are going to bring** to this role that maybe someone from this field already might not have—like maybe you are an especially creative problem-solver. Think about **what** you would need to do next and **HOW** you would do it.

Key to a Great Interview!

A 30-60-90-day plan helps make it an easy decision to hire you!

Find out more about 30-60-90-Day Plans at http://CareerConfidential.com

When you talk about your next 30 days (the 90-day part), show this hiring manager **how you will be moving on your own to benefit the company and succeed in your role**. What will you be doing? (Base this on what you have learned from the **job description**.)

The more **research** you can do for your plan, the more you will be able to show that you are very **capable of doing this job even if you have little to no experience**.

As a bonus, creating a plan shows that you're an **incredibly motivated, energetic worker** with **strategic thinking skills**, **prioritization skills**, and **plenty of initiative** and **will to succeed**.

If for some reason after walking them through your plan, they still are pushing you on the experience factor, say:

"Well, everyone has to start somewhere. No one starts every job with all the experience they need. Did you have any experience in your first job? And yet you are very successful. I would say that even though I don't have experience yet, my plan shows you that I am tremendously motivated and I believe that the skill sets I'm bringing from my previous jobs will make me a versatile asset in this role."

Key to a Great Interview

Job Shadowing

If you are new to a career, a job shadowing experience gives you more "meat" to talk about during the interview. You're going to have more understanding of a typical day on the job and what the challenges and issues will be. That helps you speak more intelligently about what you can bring to the table, and why it's going to be a good idea to hire you. It's also going to help tremendously in creating your 30/60/90-day plan--which is vital to your interview success when transitioning careers.

Bonus:
How to Handle Illegal Interview Questions

Because of the United States' strong anti-discrimination laws, many job interview questions are actually illegal—this includes questions about your **gender, children or future children, marital status, nationality, religion, disability, and age**.

However, this doesn't stop all employers from asking them. Not all of them ask with bad intent— some are just trying to make conversation with you and maybe find common ground—but the question is inappropriate just the same and you do not have to answer it.

You don't want to come right out and tell them that what they are asking is an illegal question they

> ## My Advice...
>
> If the employer asks you one or two interview questions and allows you to successfully dodge them, then you can probably safely assume it was just a mistake on their part and let it go. If they ask many of these questions, or insist on answers they are not legally allowed, you may not want to work for that company.

have no right to know the answer to. That tends to increase the tension and create an antagonistic conversation you might not be able to turn around, and your job interview will be ruined—even if the employer actually had a high level of interest in you as a candidate.

If you can, try to tactfully dodge the question without actually answering it. Here are a few illegal interview questions with ideas for how to address them.

Questions About Gender

Usually these questions center around something like, "Do you really think you can run a team of all men?"

A good answer would just slide right past that and say:

"I am very comfortable in a management role. In my last position, my team achieved X."

Questions About Children

These are usually tied to gender, asked only of female candidates. They might say, "Do you have good childcare?" meaning, "Are you going to call in sick when you have to take care of your kids?"

You should say:

"I am absolutely committed to my professional obligations and to the people here who would depend on me."

If they say, "Are you planning on having children?" or "Are you planning on having more children?" Unless you are pregnant right at that moment, I would just say, "No." First of all, you never know what the future holds, and second of all, it's none of their business.

Questions About Marital or Family Status

Any questions about plans to marry, to stay home after you have children, or your spouse's occupation or salary are all illegal.

Employers might ask these questions to get a read on how

long you'll plan to stay at the company—but if that's their question, that should be what they ask.

In response to any future marriage or family plans, smile and say, "You know, I'm not making those kinds of plans yet. I am focused on my career, and I'm interested in growth opportunities in this company. Can you tell me more about that?"

If you're asked about your spouse's occupation, it may be in a relocation situation where they're trying to see if your spouse will be OK with moving with you. I would be OK answering that question. If your spouse is in an impressive career, their follow up question may be, "Wow, then what are you doing looking for a job?" Just smile and say, "I work for many reasons other than money. I am very talented and skilled at X, Y, and Z and I enjoy the work as well as achieving goals, like I did last year in my job where I _____." Fill in the blank with whatever outstanding and impressive thing you did.

Questions About Nationality

Sometimes this is a simple, "Where are you from?" and they don't mean any harm by it. Just smile and say, "Texas. How about you?"

Many companies are sensitive to whether or not you are legally allowed to work in the U.S., and that is a question they can ask. They can't ask "What race are you?" or "Were you born in the United States?" They can only say, "Are you legally allowed to work in the U.S.?"

If you have an accent and the interviewer says, "Oh, are you from X?" it is probably an innocent question. Your best bet is to smile and say, "Yes, I moved here X years ago and I am legally allowed to work in the U.S." If this is not your first job in the States, say, "In fact, I've been very successful working as an X for ABC Corporation."

They might say, "Is English your first language?" Feel free to say, "I speak both English and Spanish fluently." (Or whatever language you speak, of course.)

Questions About Religion

Employers are not allowed to ask about your religion, whether you're going to be asking off work for religious holidays or if you go to church on Sundays. They *can* ask if you are available to work on Sundays, or if you will be able to work normal work hours.

Just say, "I'm certain I will be able to work the schedule that is required for this position. Is there anything unusual about the schedule that I should know about?"

(I always like the tactic of asking a follow up question for clarification.)

Questions About Disability

Employers are not allowed to ask direct questions about your disability, but they can ask if you are able to perform specific job duties. If they ask anything you are not comfortable answering, you can just say, "That isn't something that will interfere with my ability to do this job."

Questions About Age

Generally, questions about age are going to be a problem (and a legal issue) for those who are over 40.

If you are asked blatantly, "How old are you?" "When did you graduate?" or "When were you born?" and you truly think they will hold it against you, say:

"My age isn't relevant as to whether or not I can do this job, but my experience is, and I have experience in X, Y, and Z. In fact, I won the award last year in my company for X." Mention some notable achievement that illustrates that you are successful and good at your job.

****

Remember, most illegal interview questions are not asked with malicious intent. Usually, they are innocent questions asked by inexperienced interviewers in an attempt to spark conversation and get to know you.

In most cases, you can tactfully dodge the question with a smile and a sentence that directs the conversation back to your fit for the job, maybe even answering the question they should have asked, but didn't.

If you genuinely feel that this question was inappropriate, and can't dodge it, you can ask how this applies to your ability to do the job.

*** Note: This section on illegal interview questions is not intended to be a comprehensive list of illegal interview questions, and does not substitute for legal advice.

If You Liked This Book, Please Give It 5 Stars!

Reader reviews are so important...both for the success of this book and for me, so I know that I have given you what you need to be wildly successful in your next interview.

If you now feel as if you can tackle your next interview with confidence, let me know!

If you put the tips and principles of this book into practice and it results in an amazing interview for you, let me know!

ADDITIONAL RESOURCE GUIDE

Free Apps for iPhone, iPad and Android

Job Interview Questions and Answers

Free interactive video app lets you **practice your answers** to tough interview questions with Peggy McKee in an easy mock interview format. **Learn more here:**
http://jobinterviewquestionsandanswersapp.com/

Resume Review Pro

Improve your resume in **less than 10 minute**s with the top 'must do' resume tips.

Learn more here: http://resumereviewproapp.com/

Job Search Tips

This comprehensive app gives you **a strong resume, attention-getting cover letters, and more interviews.**

Learn more here: http://jobsearchtipsapp.com/

Free Training Webinars

Career Confidential offers weekly online training sessions to arm you with insightful, cutting-edge tips and strategies for your **resume, job search, and interviews.**

http://careerconfidential.com/training-webinars/

More by Peggy McKee amazon.com

How to Answer Interview Questions

*(101 **additional** job interview questions and answers!)*

How Do You Prepare For an Interview?

Finding a Job Fast Using a 30 / 60 / 90 Day Plan

How to Ace Your Phone Interview

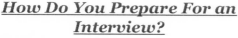

Career Confidential Products

Career Confidential is your 'go-to' resource for tools and coaching that get you HIRED. We help job seekers worldwide get jobs fast.

Explore customizable, unique, and powerful tools for a wildly successful job search here:

http://careerconfidential.com/job-search-tools/

Career Confidential Blog

Get the latest articles and tips for your job search success!

http://careerconfidential.com/blog/